Wallace & Gromit™ in THE WRONG TROUSERS™

TEACHER'S BOOK

Peter Viney and Karen Viney

Oxford University Press

1998

Oxford University Press
Great Clarendon Street, Oxford OX2 6DP

Oxford New York
Athens Auckland Bangkok Bogota Bombay
Buenos Aires Calcutta Cape Town Dar es Salaam
Delhi Florence Hong Kong Istanbul Karachi
Kuala Lumpur Madras Madrid Melbourne
Mexico City Nairobi Paris Singapore
Taipei Tokyo Toronto Warsaw

and associated companies in
Berlin Ibadan

OXFORD and OXFORD ENGLISH are
trade marks of Oxford University Press

First published 1998

ISBN 019 459029 1   Student's Book
ISBN 019 459030 5   Teacher's Book

ISBN 019 459025 9   VHS PAL Video Cassette
ISBN 019 459026 7   VHS SECAM Video Cassette
ISBN 019 459027 5   VHS NTSC Video Cassette

© Oxford University Press, 1998
Wallace and Gromit™ © Aardman/Wallace and Gromit Ltd 1993

Printed in Portugal

Acknowledgments

*The publisher would like to thank the following for their
co-operation and assistance:*
Liz Keynes, Tracey Small and Andrea Redfern
    of Aardman Animations Ltd.

Adaptation based on Nick Park's *The Wrong Trousers* produced by
    Aardman Animations for the BBC.

Adaptor's acknowledgment
The adaptors would like to thank the following people at Oxford
University Press for their commitment and enthusiasm:
Rob Maidment, who produced the ELT adaptation
    of The Wrong Trousers..
Martyn Hobbs, who edited the ELT version.
Rob Hancock, who designed the Teacher's Book.
Timothy Blakey and Louis Harrison, who edited the Teacher's Book.

CONTENTS

To the teacher

THE WRONG TROUSERS STUDENT'S BOOK

The Student's Book contains for each of the six episodes:

• Watching the video

Four pages of activities for classroom exploitation. Though these could be done in a single classroom lesson, we recommend allowing a double lesson (90 to 100 minutes) for the exploitation of the video.

In general, the activities follow this format:

1 Viewing of the complete episode

- Pre-tasks (*Before you watch*)
- Watch the whole episode
- Post-tasks (*After you watch*)

At this level, it is best to let students see the whole episode. If you are using the video at higher levels, you might choose to exploit it section by section without this initial global viewing.

2 The episode is then divided into sections (usually four) for detailed exploitation. Each section consists of

- Pre-tasks (*Before you watch*)
- Watch the section
- *While you watch* activity (optional)
- Post-tasks (*After you watch*)

3 Watch the whole episode again

It's very important to let students watch the whole episode again, so that they can feel how much their comprehension has increased as a result of the exploitation tasks. This may be followed by a post task.

If you simply follow the activities suggested, you will have a thorough exploitation of the materials.

If you have more time with video, you can add some of the activities suggested below under Teaching with video: some techniques.

• Exercises

The Exercises and Transfer will provide another one to two lessons of work based on the story of each episode.

The Exercises are related to the story of the video, but can be done after the initial exploitation, without access to video equipment. If time is short, the Exercises page can be done as homework.

1 First there is a *Memory* exercise to review the content of the episode.

2 This is followed by a *Test yourself* section which students should self-correct by reading the Transcripts. This encourages students to use the Transcripts in an active manner.

3 A structural exercise usually comes third.

4 Finally, there is an exercise on sounds / spelling.

Optionally, you can replay the video to check these exercises if equipment is available.

• Transfer

Transfer activities enable students to use the material from the video in a way that is personally meaningful. These involve paired practice.

Often, we set up a simple information gap by asking students to change partners after an initial paired question and answer session. They then ask and answer about their previous partners.

Structurally, this means shifting from 1st and 2nd person work (*I, you*) to third person work (*she, he*).

Communicatively, it means asking questions where they genuinely do not know the answer. One student has information to share with her or his partner.

• Vocabulary

This section can be used at any time during work on a particular video for reference, or later as further exercises with a vocabulary bias. There are cross-references to Vocabulary where relevant.

• Grammar

A complete language summary of each video is given for reference. There are cross-references to grammar throughout the exploitation sequences.

• Transcripts

We recommend that these should not be used in class, but in our experience the great majority of students wish to have a transcript to which they can refer **after** the lesson. We have found that students make copious notes and add translations to transcripts of videos, and this is usually done at home, on their own. Such extra work can only be advantageous, even though most experienced video teachers would opt strongly for discouraging their use before viewing. They are encouraged to use the Transcripts to check the *Test yourself* section in the Exercises.

Level

The video has been designed at beginner level. The student's book aims for a 'neutral' interpretation so as to make it suitable for the widest possible age range. In other words, we have avoided emphasis on the 'younger' aspects of the characters (such as Wallace and Gromit cuddly toys!), while also avoiding any activities that excluded the younger learner in terms of sophistication of approach or using life experience.

It is an adaptation of an Academy Award-winning animated film by Nick Park, written by Nick Park and Bob Baker. The visuals, music and sound effects are identical. However, in this ELT version, the language level of the dialogue has been greatly simplified and a narrator has been added. As adaptors we were aware of an awesome responsibility. The original is so well loved and so highly rated that it was difficult to start again from scratch. After extensive research, it was decided to keep the language level as low as we possibly could in this version, and to confine it almost entirely to the present tenses with the addition of *was* and *were* from Episode 3 onward.

The video can be used at virtually all levels by amending the tasks. The tasks in this version are at beginner level, but assume that at least a term's work has been covered.

By confining the tasks we have been unable to explore many of the possibilities, such as Gromit's wonderful body language which would allow the teacher to ask about Gromit's feelings. We have avoided the past tense (except for *was* and *were*), which with higher classes would greatly enrich review activities between episodes. We have avoided much of the language of speculation which would have added prediction activities.

We have, however, suggested some of the possibilities for extension in the teacher's notes which follow.

Instructional language

We have had to decide whether to use language for exercise instructions at the level of students at each point in the course, or whether to use instructions beyond their language level. We feel that totally confining instructions to the student level in exploiting the video would restrict the type of activities we could suggest too much. We have therefore addressed the instructions for activities at slightly above the perceived student level. The possibilities with video are such that we think it worth the teacher getting more complex instructions across to the students. Ideally this would be done by demonstration and example initially. As a last resort, they may be translated.

Using *The Wrong Trousers* as supplementary material

The Wrong Trousers can be used as a supplement to any beginner / elementary course. If it is done quickly, and extra discussion generated from the Teacher's notes it can be used at higher levels also.

Using *The Wrong Trousers* on its own

The Wrong Trousers may be used as a free-standing short course, taking anywhere between twelve and thirty classroom hours to complete.

It may be useful as a short introductory course in situations where pupils have come from different schools or classes, and have differing levels of English. As a short, easy course, it will help to consolidate a general body of knowledge. This means it is ideal where pupils have changed schools, say from Middle to Lower Secondary or from Lower Secondary to Upper Secondary.

It may be also useful as material to complete a year's work.

It has proved equally popular with adults.

A note on gender

The Wrong Trousers was originally designed as an entertainment programme for a general native-speaker audience. There happen to be three male characters in the story, but no females. We have been concerned to redress the balance. We have tried to do so by putting *she* examples first in Grammar and Transfer exercises, or where there is only one example in a Transfer exercise, giving a feminine example.

THE VIDEO RECORDER CONTROLS

Play (>)

Plays the video tape.
Note: On some machines you press PLAY to release PAUSE. On others you press PAUSE again.

Stop (■)

Stops the video tape. The picture switches off.

The TV may revert to a blank screen or to a TV channel. We advise leaving the TV set on a blank channel, or on a video channel if there is a seperate button.

It is also advisable to locate a minor control on the TV or video which switches between LINE (the video only) and TUNER (which tunes in the TV channels). If you select LINE, the TV should display a blank screen when you press STOP. Alternatively, where the TV is only ever used for video work you may choose not to connect it to a TV aerial.

Pause / Still / Freeze frame (II)

Pauses or freeze frames the video tape. Note on some machines you press PLAY to release PAUSE. On others you press PAUSE again. This is one of the most important controls on a video for classroom use. Ideally, you should be able to operate this function with the remote control.

Freeze frame will not harm the videotape. All VCR's are designed to release the freeze frame automatically before any damage can be done. Freeze frame is the most important feature on video players in the classroom, and should be the main criterion in selecting a particular make of machine.

A remote control is probably the next most important item.

Most modern machines (i.e. post 1989) have near perfect freeze frame, so look out for names like SUPER STILL, or PERFECT STILL on recorders. If there is picture wobble, the still picture quality can be changed by adjusting the TRACKING control on the video player.

Older machines have pictures which may wobble when paused and have white lines. The irritation of these can be alleviated by pressing the freeze frame control once or twice, moving the white line to a less important part of the picture. A few light taps on the machine will often move the white line on older machines.

Rewind (<<) / Fast forward (>>)

There are two types of REWIND (<<) and FAST FORWARD (>>) on most machines.

The ones labelled REWIND / FAST FORWARD will normally blank out the picture.

Ones labelled CUE / REVIEW or PICTURE SEARCH will enable the picture to be seen at speed during rewinding and fast forward operation. Apart from being useful for finding the place, these facilities can be used to remind students of parts of the story.

Still advance (I>)

Video tape in the PAL (UK, Germany, Europe) or SECAM (France, parts of Eastern Europe and Latin America) formats has 25 pictures (frames) per second. NTSC tape (in the USA, Canada, Mexico and East Asia) has 30 frames per second. Still Advance allows you to move the video on by one frame at a time. This is vastly more accurate than simply pushing PAUSE. Note: You may find that several frames have almost no movement, while others are dramatic changes of picture.

Jog/Shuttle

This is an editing facility which can be found on more sophisticated videos. It is a rotary control which enables you to move the picture forwards or backwards as if by hand at various speeds. If this control is fitted, it is extremely useful in the classroom. It is well worth seeking this facility when purchasing new equipment. However, note that it is rarely available on the remote control.

Mute

This control is situated on most TV remote controls (Note: TV control, not video control). It immediately removes (or 'mutes') the soundtrack. By pressing it again, you restore the sound at the preset level. Because its effect is instant, it is much easier to use in the classroom than the volume control for the TV.

Locating the place on the tape

There are three or four sections in each episode. The sections are labelled on the Transcripts pages.

The Student's Book assumes that your video has a minutes and seconds counter. The timing is noted for each episode in the section headings. You will have to zero the counter at the start of each episode. There should be a RESET or ZERO COUNTER button on your video or remote control to enable you to do this.

Press RESET during the written screen titles and release it just as they disappear. You can use a watch or a clock where the video does not have a minutes and seconds timer.

You may wish to record the counter number (or time reference in minutes and seconds on newer video machines) for the beginning of each video on the contents pages.

If you have an older three or four digit counter, record the numbers for each section of the videos in your copy of the Student's Book.

If your machine has MEMORY REWIND (or REPEAT), you can reset the counter at various points in the lesson. This control will rewind the tape as far as zero whenever REWIND is selected.

TEACHING WITH VIDEO:
Some techniques

Silent viewing activities

Silent viewing means turning off the sound on the TV or monitor and making use of the visuals on their own. This is most easily accomplished with the MUTE control (see above). Silent viewing will be a PREDICTION technique when students are viewing for the first time, and a REPRODUCTION technique when they have already seen and heard the section being used for silent viewing.

a Prediction

Students can talk about EVENTS (*What's happening on the screen?*) or DIALOGUE (*What are they saying?*)

They will be able to predict dialogue, i.e. guess what people are saying, throughout the course.

b Reproduction

Reproduction (or retelling) can also be divided into REPRODUCTION OF DIALOGUE and REPRODUCTION OF EVENTS. Reproduction of dialogue might be most effective where there are useful formulas, fixed expressions and points of intonation or pronunciation. Reproduction of events tends to focus on narrative tenses and on sequences.

c Random sound down (Cloze listening)

This may be done at any time, but is particularly suitable when viewing the whole episode again. Turn the sound down or mute the sound at random intervals asking students to fill in the missing dialogue.

Sound only activities

You can play a section of one of the videos with the picture turned off so that they hear the dialogue but are unable to see the action. This can be done by using the brightness controls on the television, by unplugging the picture connectors (BNC or yellow phono leads, on sets where sound and picture have separate leads) or most simply by placing something in front of the screen, such as a jacket or a sheet of cardboard.

Students can be asked either to predict what is happening visually, or to use the dialogue as a memory spur to recall what happened visually.

See *Random sound down* above. A parallel activity can also be done by obscuring the picture with card at random intervals.

Freeze framing (still picture) activities

Freeze framing means stopping the picture, using the FREEZE FRAME, STILL or PAUSE (❚❚ or >❙<) control.

FRAME ADVANCE or STILL ADVANCE is a very useful control found on some modern machines, moving the still picture forward one frame at a time. It can be used to explore the nuances of an event or of a facial reaction.

a Prediction

Prediction occurs when freeze framing is used during the initial viewing of a section. You can freeze frame and ask about either EVENTS (*What's going to happen?*) or DIALOGUE (*What are they saying? / What are they going to say next?*). See Silent Viewing above.

b Reproduction

When students have already seen a section, they will be using memory to reproduce either what is being said, or to describe what is happening, or what has just happened.

c Using the background

Video contains 25 pictures per second (or 30 in NTSC areas), and there is a wealth of detail in the background of the pictures which can be exploited by freeze framing. Teachers can often find something new even when they have done a particular lesson many times. The background also gives access to material about British life and culture.

One of the main differences between videos designed for educational broadcast and videos designed for classroom use lies in the presumption of the teacher's ability to use freeze frame to explore and exploit background detail. The camera does not need to linger on things in the background, they can always be singled out later with the freeze frame control.

d Thoughts and emotions

Video gives us an additional dimension of information about characters' body language, facial expressions, gesture, stance, reaction and response. This information can be exploited in the classroom. Freeze frame and ask about feelings and emotions. Gromit is wonderfully expressive without speaking. In some activities students can deduce further information about the characters, based on what they have picked up from the video, but requiring the use of their imagination.

Paired viewing activities

Paired activities take more effort in setting up, but the results justify the trouble.

a Description

In this activity one student in each pair turns their back to the screen. The other student faces the screen, and the video is played silently. The student who can see the screen describes what they can see to their partner.

Both students will wish to hear the dialogue later.

The 'passive' student in each pair will be motivated to see what they have missed as well! It is worth making sure that the partners swop roles, or that the activity is done twice, with different sections so that each partner gets a chance to perform the 'active' role.

b Narration

This is more difficult to organise, as it involves sending half the class out of the room while the remaining half watch a section of a video. When they return, they are told about the video in pairs by those who saw it. (See the note above about swopping roles.) In school situations, this can be done by team teaching, and working with two parallel classes at the same time.

c Split class: Description / Narration

Half the class is sent out. The remainder watch a section silently. Then the two halves swop places. The ones that were outside now listen to the same section with the picture covered (See: Sound only, above.) The students are then paired off. One student in each pair has **seen** the video, but hasn't heard the dialogue. The other student has only **heard** the dialogue. They work together to piece the story together.

Role-plays / T.P.R.

Students can be asked to role-play sequences they have seen in any videos.

We have found it more interesting to get them to role play things which are **not** seen in the video, but which they can guess from having seen the video. Role-play is of limited use with *The Wrong Trousers* as there is no model of two-part dialogue in the story.

However, T.P.R activities (Total Physical Response) are possible. The teacher (or a student) reads the narrator's parts. Students role-play Wallace, Gromit and the penguin and mime the actions in response to the reading. This works well where students are shy of speaking in English. They demonstrate comprehension by their actions. This gives confidence. While it always works well with younger students, we would also encourage you to try it if you are teaching an older group.

FURTHER WORK

The Aardman world wide web

Aardman is the company which produced *The Wrong Trousers*. Where the school or students at home have internet access, we highly recommend accessing the Aardman web site at:

http://www.aardman.com

Note: This site is related to the original, non-simplified version of *The Wrong Trousers* and also has information on other Aardman productions including *A Close Shave* and the forthcoming series *Rex the Runt*.

Reference

The recommended dictionaries at the level are *The Oxford Picture Dictionary* and *The Oxford Elementary Learner's Dictionary of English*. Even at this early level, it is worth encouraging the use of a monolingual dictionary, though most students will wish to use a bilingual dictionary as a second resort. Encourage them to use a monolingual dictionary first, and a bilingual dictionary only if they haven't understood the monolingual explanation.

The Grammar pages in the Student's Book should be sufficient on their own without using a seperate grammar reference book.

The original videos

Where students are at a higher level, you may wish to give them the opportunity of comparing this ELT version with the authentic original version (published by the BBC).

A Grand Day Out / A Close Shave

The Wrong Trousers is the second of three films starring Wallace and Gromit. All three are available in the original versions on video (BBC), and may be available in translation.

THE VIDEO CLASSROOM

We have found that most video equipment in schools is linked to TV sets or monitors by the simplest method, using the aerial sockets. This is a pity when most modern equipment has either separate video (BNC or YELLOW PHONO) and audio sockets (RED AND WHITE PHONO or DIN), or in much of Europe, a 21 pin SCART connector, or (with Hi-Band machines, such as S-VHS machines) special S-VHS connectors for picture.

The use of these connections should almost always bring about a significant improvement in both picture and audio quality. Try it! See the manufacturer's handbooks for your equipment. A copy of these should be kept with the equipment in case of problems. Incidentally, the most common difficulty we have found is that many of the latest TV sets revert to Channel 1 when they are switched off, often making it necessary to reselect the video channel. This does not matter when the VCR is connected by means of a SCART connector.

Another common irritation is noise, and white lines on the blank screen when the VCR is stopped. This can be eliminated by selecting LINE or AV on the VCR rather than TUNER. There will then be no need to switch the television off between activities.

Precautions

You should always pay attention to sight lines in the classroom and ensure that everyone can see the screen well. This may seem obvious, but we have done video demonstrations where someone has complained (always afterwards) that their view was obscured! In many classrooms, reflected sunlight can cause problems.

Video equipment should be positioned so as not to expose it to chalk dust. The ink dust from marker pens is less intrusive, but still harmful if the board is right above the video machine.

Video tapes store their signal magnetically. They can be damaged by exposure to extremes of temperature (such as being left on a radiator, or in a hot car) and by magnets and electric fields. The speakers in TV sets contain magnets, and the tubes generate an electric field. The video may be damaged by leaving it on top of a TV set or external speaker.

BACKGROUND NOTES

This information is for the teacher. It is up to you to decide how much you want to explain to your class. You needn't explain any of it if you don't want to. We would not in most situations. But we feel that you should have this information available.

If you are a native speaker of English, you should skip this section entirely!

Technical notes

The Wrong Trousers was animated by Nick Park, and has won the Academy award for best short animated film. It took ten people fourteen months to make, The characters are made of Plasticine moulded over a metal frame with moveable joints. There are about 42,000 individual still pictures in the film (and you can access any one of them by using the pause control).

Cultural notes

The story is set in a small industrial town in the north of England. Wallace's redbrick house is about one hundred years old, and this kind of house can be found in any British town.

The setting is very typical of Britain. The soap opera, *Coronation Street* which has dominated British TV since 1959 has a similar redbrick, industrial town setting, again in the north of England. People used to joke about the decoration of rooms in *Coronation Street*. They had floral wallpaper and the trademark was the three plaster 'flying ducks' on the wall. You will notice that Wallace has similar 'flying rockets' on his wall. He's an inventor, and the first Wallace and Gromit animation, *A Grand Day Out* involves a rocket trip to the Moon.

The most popular British children's comics, *Beano* and *Dandy* (which are produced in Scotland) date back to the late 1930s. They are set in similar streets, somewhere in Northern England or Scotland. They also feature animals functioning in a human world (their early characters were Korky the Kat and Biffo The Bear.) Part of the appeal of Wallace and Gromit has been their distinctive Britishness.

Teachers will ask how typical the setting is. The rooms and styles are deliberately very much 1950s /1960s Britain. More people probably live in modern houses in suburbs nowadays, but this is an older urban environment which students would still see anywhere in Britain.

Accents

Regions

Wallace has a Yorkshire accent. He is played both in the original version, and in this ELT Adaptation by Peter Sallis, an actor famous as a Yorkshireman in the long-running British sitcom *Last of The Summer Wine.*

The story is narrated by Stephen Tompkinson, who speaks in a Lancashire accent. Lancashire is on the west side of the Pennine mountains (Manchester and Liverpool are the biggest cities). Yorkshire is on the east side of the Pennines (Leeds, Sheffield, Hull and York are its best-known cities). Both of them have Northern accents, which have been retained.

Pronunciation

Until recently, British English teaching was dominated by an accent called 'RP' or 'Received Pronunciation' which was the educated English of the south (though some linguists now believe that it is being replaced by 'Estuary English' – the accent of English east and south of London). Northern vowel sounds in words like *bath*, *laugh*, *castle* and *can't* have the same short 'a' sound as in American English. In fact, many more speakers of English in the world use this short 'a' sound than use the long 'a' of RP, which sounds like 'barth', 'ear-stle' and 'earn't'. The accents are part of the integral style of the story. In case anyone thinks we have a mission to change the world, we should state right away that both adaptors are Southerners who naturally use the RP long 'a' in their own speech. One of the problems of paying great attention to teaching a very narrow range of vowel sounds is the wide diversity of vowel sounds found among native speakers of English. We have always believed that students must be exposed to a variety of accents from the very beginning.

Stress

You will observe that Wallace uses a typical Yorkshire stress pattern in speech, in giving almost equal weight to syllables in many words. Students will actually find this easier to understand than an accent which has greater difference in weight between syllables. For example, Wallace says *birth-<u>day</u>* with near equal stress. A strong RP accent would stress the first syllable, '<u>birth</u>-day'.

Remember, there is no such thing as 'a correct accent'. Experience indicates that the mother tongue has much greater influence on the students' eventual accent in English than the accent of the teacher or of the recorded materials.

Peter Viney & Karen Viney
Poole, Dorset

Meet

Wallace and Gromit

Before you watch episode one

This section is used before any work starts on the video. Focus attention on the table and give students time to read it.

Have students cover the text, and ask the questions to the class.

> **Higher levels**
> You may wish to skip this section altogether, or you can go through at speed, using additional / alternative questions.
> e.g. *Where do you live? What do you do?*

1 My name's (Jack). Ask and answer these questions.

Put students into pairs. As this is the first paired activity in the course we suggest taking extra care when setting this up. Make sure students know what they are supposed to do. Note they can ask and answer one question at a time, or Student A can ask all five questions, followed by Student B asking all five questions.

What's your first name?
What's your favourite food?
What's your family name?
What's your favourite drink?
What's your address?

e.g.
My first name's Maria. My family name's Smith.

2 Change partners. Ask and answer questions about your first partner.

By changing pairs, students move from 1st (*I, we*) and 2nd (*you*) person practice to 3rd person (*she, he, it*) practice. This will be a regular activity throughout the book. It is worth setting up pairs and 'pairs to change to' carefully the first time, so that it can be done quickly as the book progresses.

What's (her/his) first name?
What's (her/his) favourite food?
What's (her/his) family name?
What's (her/his) favourite drink?
What's (her/his) address?

e.g.
His first name's Paul. Her first name's Anna.

> See: Grammar, page 12, 4 Singular possessive adjectives

Cross-references to *Grammar* appear throughout the book. Show students where to find the grammar notes, and go through them if necessary.

Gromit's birthday

Watching the video

Watch all of episode one.

We suggest watching the whole episode initially so that students can experience how much (or how little) they can understand of an extended piece.

After you watch

1 Number these pictures in order from one to twelve.

one 1	four 4	seven 7	ten 10
two 2	five 5	eight 8	eleven 11
three 3	six 6	nine 9	twelve 12

Have students work individually to complete the task.

Answers

K 1 / E 2 / J 3 / C 4 / F 5 / I 6 / A 7 / B 8 / L 9 / G 10 / D 11 / H 12

2 Make sentences in pairs.

first	second	third	fourth	fifth	sixth
seventh	eighth	ninth	tenth	eleventh	twelfth

● *B is sixth.*
■ *No, it isn't sixth. It's seventh.*

This moves from cardinal numbers (*one, two,* etc.) to ordinal numbers (*first, second,* etc.). If students have difficulty, have them repeat *seven – seventh*, etc. You can write up:

A – 7, B – 7th

Then the teacher says cardinal or ordinal numbers aloud. The students call out *A* (cardinal) or *B* (ordinal).

T: 6 / 8th / 9th / 6 / 6th / 4 / 8 / 4th / 9 / 6th … etc.

(Repeat numbers to make it challenging.)

Be careful with the spelling of *fifth* and *twelfth*.

3 Say aloud:

1 Have students repeat the letters in groups after you.

Note: The groups are arranged according to British English pronunciation. In American English, *Z* (UK: zed; US: zee) moves from the *F/L/M …* group to the *B/C/D…* group. The sample words have been chosen because they all appear in the video.

2 Write the letters on the board and point at random for individual students to pronounce the letter.

3 Have students spell their names aloud.

name ... A ... H ... J ... K

tea ... B ... C ... D ... E ... G ... P... T ... V

express ... F ... L ... M ... N ... S ... X ... Z

my ... I ... Y

toast ... O

you ... Q ... U ... W

card ... R

SECTION ONE　　00.00 to 01.10

Before you watch

1 Do you know these words?

an egg
a calendar
a pen
a watch
a television
a birthday card
an alarm clock
a glass
a bed

Students work individually or in pairs. Check, but don't
explain the meanings yet.

Watch section one.

While you watch

2 What can you see in section one? Tick (✔) the words in the list above.

Ask the class to tell you which words were in the video.
This is open to discussion (many won't notice Gromit's
watch for example). Don't give them the idea that there's
a 'right' answer in this kind of exercise – it's a matter of
observation. Don't give definite answers yet. This comes
in 4.

After you watch

3 Answer these questions.

What's the date?
What's the time?
Who is the birthday card from?

Answers
February 12th / The 12th of February / It's the 12th of
　February.
Nine o'clock / It's nine o'clock.
Wallace. / It's from Wallace.

Note: We write *12 February* or *12th February* but we say
the twelfth **of** February, or February **the** twelfth.
In American English, *February twelfth* (without **the**) is
more common.

4 Ask and answer questions. Use words from the list in 1.

● *Is there a teapot?*
■ *Yes, there is.*
● *Is there a spoon?*
■ *No, there isn't.*

Put students into pairs. Ensure that they understand the
task. Circulate, checking that they are taking it in turns
to ask questions.

Check by asking individual students.

e.g.
T: Is there an alarm clock? / Is there an egg? etc.

If there is disagreement, you can go back through the
section, either at normal speed or by cueing across the
video heads (speeded-up picture).

5 Look at the calendar.

Mon – Monday	Fri – Friday
Tues – Tuesday	Sat – Saturday
Wed – Wednesday	Sun – Sunday
Thurs – Thursday	

● *What day is the twelfth?*
■ *The twelfth is a Wednesday.*

Ask and answer questions about these days.

3rd / 25th / 19th / 13th / 21st / 29th / 2nd

If necessary, do choral repetition on the days of the
week. Check that they don't stress *day* (*Tuesday* **not**
Tuesday). Then have students work in pairs, referring to
the calendar. *Mon, Tues*, etc. are abbreviations.

6 Think! What month is Gromit's birthday?

Someone should tell you immediately. If not, ask them
to look at the calendar (29 days. It's February.).
You might want to explain that it's also a leap year.
If necessary, do choral repetition on the months.

e.g.
T: It's the fifth month.
Students: It's May.
T: It's the eleventh month.
Students: It's November. etc.

Note: The birthday card plays the tune *Happy Birthday
to You*. Do the class know this in English?

See: Transfer, page 9, 1 Birthdays

SECTION TWO   01:10 to 01:57

While you watch

1 Number these sentences from 1 to 5.

Answers
2 It's a long way down from upstairs.
5 Is there any post, Gromit?
1 How are you this morning then, Gromit?
4 Cracking toast, Gromit!
3 It's a big drop.

Check by asking *Which is the first sentence?*. Students reply with: *How are you this morning, Gromit?*

Notes:
1) *Cracking toast* – cracking is a regionalism, meaning *excellent* or *very good*. It's what Wallace says in the original version, and it is on Wallace & Gromit T-shirts and other merchandise. Though it is unusual, we decided to retain it as it gives atmosphere. It is **not** highly frequent. We would usually say *Great toast* or *Nice toast*.
2) Wallace has *jam* on his toast (American English: *jelly*).

Watch section two.

After you watch

2 Tick (✔) the correct answers.

Answers
1 Wallace's bedroom is (downstairs ✔upstairs).
2 Wallace has got a pain in his (✔back head).
3 Gromit (✔isn't happy is happy).
4 'Cracking' means (bad ✔good).

After students have completed the answers, you can check by asking questions.

e.g.
T: Is Wallace's bedroom downstairs?
Student 1: No, it isn't.
T: Is Wallace's bedroom upstairs?
Student 2: Yes, it is.

Note: The typical British house has two floors with bedrooms upstairs.

You may wish to explain again that Wallace is an *inventor* and that the house is full of his *inventions*. We think it is important that some words are supplied by the teacher, not just by the textbook. So, note that his inventions are *gadgets*. *Robot* is a useful way of describing the machine that dresses Wallace.

Higher levels
Modify the checking process by using question generators.
e.g.
T: Is Wallace's bedroom downstairs?
Student 1: No, it isn't.
T: Ask 'Where?'
Student 2: Where is Wallace's bedroom?
(T indicates S3)
Student 3: It's upstairs.

SECTION THREE   01.57 to 02.50

Before you watch

1 Look at the word map.

Students are not expected to do anything with the word map at this stage except look at it.

Watch section three.

After you watch

2 Complete the sentences with words from the word map.

Answers
1 Wallace's letters are all bills.
2 Wallace and Gromit have got a money problem.
3 The safe is behind the picture.
4 The piggy bank is inside the safe.
5 How much money have they got?
6 They've only got a few pence.
7 Birthday presents aren't cheap, they're expensive.

Have students work individually. They might then compare with a partner. You might elicit the answers by choosing individuals to give you their sentences.
e.g.
T: 1.
Student: Wallace's letters are all bills.

3 Add these words to the word map.

dollars / a bank / a wallet / pounds / cents

Higher levels
Ask students to add other words freely to the word map.
e.g.
cheap – inexpensive
pence – other well-known currencies (yen, franc, mark, etc.)
bills – cheques, credit cards, statements
safe – money belt, purse
This can be as open as they wish.

SECTION FOUR   02.50 to 03.46

Watch section four.

After you watch

1 Write the sentences on the correct pictures.

Answers
Happy birthday, chuck! – Picture 6
Open it, Gromit! – Picture 3
Put it on. – Picture 2
It's a lead and a collar. – Picture 5
Everyone knows you've got an owner, now. – Picture 4
Watch out, Gromit! – Picture 1

Note: *chuck* is a regionalism. It's a general term of affection.

Watch all of episode one again.

2 Tell the story of episode one. Use the pictures on this page and on page 4 to help you.

This is a very free activity where students have the opportunity to experiment with language (and this means making mistakes). If they just say one thing about each picture, that's fine. Don't expect any kind of connected narrative at this point: *It's a present. It's pink*, may be all they need to say. We would suggest being gentle with correction so as to encourage students to say as much as they can manage. The important point is that they are trying to say something in English about each picture. Pairwork is less daunting than whole class work, and you may want to have them attempt it in pairs or small groups before getting suggestions from the whole class.

> **Higher levels**
> You can obviously expect a greater range of vocabulary and structure, and it can be done in pairs, with one or two pairs selected to give a model story to the class.

Exercises

1 Memory
Are these sentences true (✔) or false (✗)?

Answers
1 Today is Wallace's birthday. ✗
2 There are five letters. Four are for Gromit, and one is for Wallace. ✗
3 Gromit's birthday card is in a green envelope. ✔
4 Wallace has got a red pullover and a green tie. ✔
5 Wallace and Gromit have got a money problem. ✔
6 The first present is on the 5.09 express train. ✗
7 There is blue wrapping paper with a gold ribbon on the first present. ✗
8 The lead and collar are grey. ✗
9 Gromit is afraid of the second birthday present. ✔

Now correct the false sentences.

Answers
1 Today is Gromit's birthday.
2 There are six letters. Five are for Wallace and one is for Gromit.
6 The first present is on the 9.05 express train.
7 There is pink wrapping paper with a gold ribbon on the first present.
8 The lead and the collar are red.

> **Higher levels**
> Check that students stress the corrected word. This is in bold above.
> e.g.The false sentence is *Today is Wallace's birthday*. The corrected sentence is *Today is Gromit's birthday*.
> Compare: If the false sentence is *Today isn't Gromit's birthday*, the corrected sentence would stress *Today is Gromit's birthday*. If the false sentence is *Tomorrow is Gromit's birthday*, the corrected sentence would be *Today is Gromit's birthday*.
> Have students try all three.

2 Test yourself
Choose the correct word in (brackets).

Answers
1 I've (got / get) a pain in my back.
2 (Are / Is) there any post?
3 Maybe we can (to rent / rent) that room out.
4 How much money (have / has) you got?
5 We've (all /only) got a few pence.
6 Everyone (know / knows) you've got an owner now.
7 You've got another present, (too / two).
8 Come and look in (here / there).
9 What is it? It's (awake / alive).

Now check with the Transcript on page 13.

3 Contractions
These contractions are in episode one.

it's	I've	we've	they're
aren't	you've	what's	

it's = it is
I've = I have

Answers
we have / they are / are not / you have / what is

> **Higher levels**
> Ask students to create example sentences for each contraction.

See: Grammar, page 12, 2 *to be*, 3 *have got / has got*

4 Sounds
In this episode, the spelling *ea* has got three different sounds:

Encourage students to say the words **aloud in their heads** and to work individually, then compare with a partner. Note: In British English *lever* is in Group A (sounds like *tea*), but in American English it's in Group B (sounds like *ready*). We don't suggest explaining this unless you are American and find the British pronunciation odd!

Put these other words in the correct sound groups: A, B or C.

me yes twelfth asleep near we be here well lever

Answers
A	B	C
tea / cheap	breakfast / ready	dear / near / here
me / asleep /	yes / twelfth / well	
we / be /		
lever / lead		

> **Higher levels**
> We would not recommend using phonetics with beginners unless you are very committed to their use and are thoroughly in command of phonetic transcriptions. If you are, then this would be a place to bring them in.

Transfer

In the Transfer section, students talk about their own experience using the language forms from the video. This involves pairwork, and in particular changing partners to get third person practice (while talking about their previous partner).

1 Birthdays
Work with a partner. Ask and answer questions, and complete the chart.

my partner	his/her father	his/her mother	his/her brother or his/her friend	his/her sister or his/her friend

- ● When's your birthday?
- ■ My birthday's January 25th (January the twenty fifth).
- ● When's your father's birthday?
- ■ His birthday's July 2nd (July the second).
- ● When's your mother's birthday?
- ■ Her birthday's February 3rd (February the third).

Have students repeat the examples chorally, then check individuals. Note the possessive ('s) – *mother's / father's / brother's / sister's / friend's* (birthday).

We assume they know basic family relationships. If there is a problem, draw a / your family tree on the board. You can use male / female symbols to clarify (or just F and M).

During the pairwork, students should note their partner's answers on their chart (or on a sheet of paper).

2 Change partners. Ask and answer questions about his/her first partner.

Students now use the notes that they have made.

e.g. The first partner was (Maria), so the sequence will become:
- ● *When's her birthday?*
- ■ *Her birthday's May the fifteenth.*
- ● *When's her mother's birthday?*
- ■ *Her mother's birthday's December the twenty-second.*

> **Higher levels**
> You could ask about the dates of important festivals or national holidays relevant to the students' own experience.

3 What colour is it? Look at the box.

pen	bag	alarm	clock	T-shirt
book	calculator	jacket	pencil	watch
notebook				

If students need to revise colours, move forward to page 11 and practise the colours chorally first.

Write four sentences.

Each student writes four true sentences.

e.g.
I've got a blue pen.
I've got a yellow alarm clock.
I've got a white T-shirt.
I've got a black bag.

> See: Vocabulary, page 11, 3 Colours

4 Ask and answer questions.

- ● Have you got a pen?
- ■ Yes, I have. / No, I haven't.
- ● What colour's your (pen)?
- ■ My pen's (blue).

This is done freely. We suggest encouraging students to ask you for the word if they have other items with them that they can use (comb, ruler, briefcase, etc.).

5 Change partners. Ask and answer questions about his/her first partner.

- ● Has she got a bag?
- ■ Yes, she has. / No, she hasn't.
- ● What colour's her bag?
- ■ Her bag's (black).

They should be able to remember (or even see) the answers! In classroom situations, remember that primary colours are less useful than colours like beige, brown, grey, cream, etc. – teach them as necessary.

> See: Grammar, page 12, 3 have got / has got

You could refer to the Grammar reference section on page 12 at this point or later. The basic problem (before going into anything else) is to establish the mechanical relationships – *he / she / it* to *has*; *we, you, they, I* to *have*. This is a situation where some rapid simple substitution drills can establish confidence.

e.g.
T: He.
Students: He's got a new car.

T: They.
Students: They've got a new car.

Continue: She / We / They / I / He / You

Vocabulary

1 In the post
Label the items with words from the box.

postcard	wrapping	paper	present
stamp	birthday	card	parcel
letter	ribbon	bill	

Answers
1 parcel
2 bill
3 birthday card
4 wrapping paper
5 present
6 letter
7 ribbon
8 postcard
9 stamp

2 On the table

This exercise should be self-explanatory. Check that students are doing it successfully.

Read this. Look at the bold words. Put them in the correct boxes on the picture.

It's breakfast time. There's a pink **toaster** in the middle of the table. Wallace has got a **yellow cup** and Gromit has got a **blue cup**. The **teapot** is brown. The **table** is brown, too. The **tablecloth** is white. There are silver **salt and pepper** pots on the table.

Answers

teapot		toaster
blue cup		yellow cup
table	salt and pepper	tablecloth

3 Colours
What are the colours? Write them in the correct order from top to bottom. Use the words in the box.

white	red	blue	yellow	pink
grey	orange	green	black	brown

Answers (from top to bottom)

pink / red / orange / yellow / green / blue / brown / white / grey / black

4 Vocabulary notebook
Write translations. You can use your dictionary.

In most cases students will gain great advantage by using a monolingual dictionary with simplified English explanations. However, at this level a bilingual dictionary is the best for this exercise. You may wish to check that the correct translations are given for the word in its context in the episode.

You may wish to write in model translations here for reference.

alive	-----------	lever	-----------
asleep	-----------	money	-----------
awake	-----------	morning	-----------
back	-----------	owner	-----------
bill	-----------	pain	-----------
birthday	-----------	picture	-----------
breakfast	-----------	post	-----------
card	-----------	present	-----------
cheap	-----------	problem	-----------
collar	-----------	ready	-----------
cup	-----------	rent	-----------
date	-----------	room	-----------
dog	-----------	safe	-----------
drop	-----------	tea	-----------
expensive	-----------	toast	-----------
jam	-----------	upstairs	-----------
lead	-----------		

Grammar

See: Student's Book, page 12

You may wish to spend time going through this. If so, we would encourage activating the student's language by introducing drills, questions, etc.

Transcript

See: Student's Book, page 13

Episode 2
Room to let

Watching the video

Before you watch

This episode introduces the Present simple, restricted to likes and dislikes. The sentences are contextualized in exercise 2 before students have to produce them in exercise 3.

1 'Room to let'
There are three bedrooms in Wallace's house. Label the pictures.

Answers
Wallace's bedroom – bottom right
Gromit's bedroom – top right
The spare bedroom – left

Wallace can't pay his bills. He has got a money problem. There is an answer. Wallace can rent a room out. Which is the 'room to let'?

Answer
The spare room

Watch all of episode two.

After you watch

2 Are these sentences true (✔) or false (✘)?

Students work individually then compare answers with a partner. Check with the class.

e.g.
T: The penguin likes the spare room. True or false?

Answers
1 The penguin likes the spare room. ✘
2 The penguin likes Gromit's room. ✔
3 Wallace doesn't like the penguin. ✘
4 Gromit likes the penguin. ✘
5 The penguin doesn't like Gromit. ✔
6 Gromit likes the techno-trousers. ✘
7 The penguin likes classical music. ✘
8 The penguin doesn't like organ music.✘
9 Gromit doesn't like organ music.✔

3 Ask and answer questions.

Pairwork. Set up pairs as in episode 1 exploitation. Students should be able to ask and answer questions for all nine sentences in 2. Check by asking the same questions to individual students selected randomly.

● Does the penguin like the spare room?
■ Yes, he does. / No, he doesn't.

Look at exercise two. Ask and answer more questions.

If students are unfamiliar with the structure, you may wish to refer forward to the Grammar section on page 22 at this point. However, we would prefer to leave this until later, allowing students a chance to work out the structure for themselves before an overt explanation.

See: Grammar, page 22, 2 Likes and dislikes

SECTION ONE	00.00 to 01.11

Before you watch

1 Write the sentences on the correct pictures.

Answers
Have a nice walk, Gromit! – top right
They're techno-trousers. – bottom right
I can't pay these bills. – centre
It's a very big present. – bottom left

Watch section one.

After you watch

2 Choose the correct answers.

In this exercise the language appears to be above the student level. Don't explain words, encourage students to make intelligent guesses.

1 N.A.S.A. means …
National Aeronautical and Space Administration ✔
New Age Soldiers' Armour

2 'walkies' means …
A radio or intercom
A walk for dogs or small children ✔

3 'Dogs must be kept on a lead' means …
Don't take the lead off your dog ✔
Don't put a lead on your dog

4 'Apply within' means …
Put your application inside a letter
Ask in this house ✔

3 Make sentences. Say them to your partner.
e.g.

Have a nice walk!

The most important point here is that students should say these lines with meaning and enthusiasm. Use choral repetition and encourage them to be expressive.

Have	a	nice	walk!
		good	day!
		lovely	holiday!
		great	time!
			weekend!
			evening!

At the end of the lesson, say one of the sentences to your teacher.

Make sure that they do!

Note: In the park you can see a slide and a swing. When Wallace is working on his bills, he's using both a calculator and an abacus.

SECTION TWO 01.12 to 02.51

Before you watch

1 Noises
Say these words aloud.

Have fun with this. Encourage the students to repeat the noises as if they were doing sound effects in a movie!

e.g.
tick-tock-tick-tock-tick-tock-tick-tock

Point out that the words seem to represent the sounds.

creak / tick tock / ring / click clack / crash / squeak / boing

Then match the noises to the pictures.

Answers
clock – tick tock
knitting needles – click clack
doorbell – ring
door – creak
picture – crash
bed – squeak
bedspring – boing

Watch section two.

While you watch

2 You can hear a lot of noises in section two. Tick (✔) the noises you hear.

knitting needles ✔
a clock ✔
a doorbell ✔
a door opening ✔
a bird singing
a door closing ✔
the penguin's feet ✔
classical music ✔
a telephone
Wallace laughing ✔
a picture falling ✔
a dog barking
a squeaky bed ✔
a bedspring ✔
organ music ✔

> **(Much) higher levels:**
> You could point out the gerundive (verbal noun) in *the sound of a picture falling*, *the sound of Wallace laughing*.

After you watch

3 Check with a partner.

Have students ask and answer questions about all the noises, then check through by asking the questions to individuals selected at random.

● *Can you hear a doorbell in section two?*
■ *Yes, I can. / No, I can't.*

4 Wallace says *three* of these sentences to the penguin. Which three? Tick (✔) them.

Come inside. ✔
Follow me. ✔
Go upstairs.
It's a long way.
It's this way. ✔

5 Complete the sentences.

Students can do this individually, or co-operatively in pairs. Check through afterwards, having students repeat the correct sentences chorally and individually.

Answers
1 There's someone at the door, Gromit.
2 Can I show you the room?
3 It's twenty pounds a week.
4 What would you like for breakfast, Penguin?
5 You can have toast and jam, or fish!
6 It's a bit dark. But I can decorate it for you.
7 No, you can't have this room. It's Gromit's.
8 There's one very important rule.
9 Now I can pay the bills.

> **Higher levels**
> Very observant students might notice the LP in Gromit's room. It's by his favourite composer, Bach (bark). You could also ask *How many times can you see bones?* (on Gromit's kitting, on the wallpaper in his room, on the picture over the bed).

Note: Wallace has advertised because he wants to rent the room out. The person who rents the room is a **lodger**, though in the original video Wallace calls them a **paying guest** which is a nicer way of saying the same thing. A lodger usually shares facilities with the people in a house. If the room has its own bathroom and kitchen, it is a **self-contained flat**. This isn't. You may wish to add these words during the lesson, though they can be avoided if you want to minimize vocabulary load.

When the penguin switches on the radio, the organ music is *Tie A Yellow Ribbon* – this is of no importance, except it can be really irritating when you recognize a tune but can't remember the title!

SECTION THREE   02.51 to 03.47

While you watch

1 Do you know these words?

Students look at the words and check either with a partner or the class as a whole. They shouldn't actually tick the boxes until *While you watch* below.

a ladder
a stepladder ✔
a hammer
a tin of paint ✔
a paintbrush ✔
a screwdriver
a roller ✔
an electric drill
a roll of wallpaper ✔
a light bulb ✔

You may not need to refer forward to Vocabulary, but if necessary refer students to page 21 and check.

> **Higher levels**
> You could note *an electric drill*. It is *a drill*, but *an electric drill*. The article agrees with the next word, in this case an adjective, not the noun.

See: Vocabulary, page 20, 3 Decorating

While you watch

Watch section three.

2 What can you see in section 3?
Tick (✔) the words in the list above.

After you watch

3 The instruction book
Look at this: 7 - 9 - 6 - 7 - 1 - 5 - 7 - 9

This means: Walk. Stop. Turn right. Walk. Leg up. Suction on. Walk. Stop.

What does this mean?

7 - 9 - 4 - 7 - 9 - 6 - 7 - 9 - 1 - 5 - 7 - 9 - 3

Answers

Walk. Stop. Turn left. Walk. Stop. Turn right. Walk. Stop. Leg up. Suction on. Walk. Stop. Leg down.

4 Your partner is in the techno-trousers.
Give your partner instructions.

This is a noisy activity. Students follow the instructions by performing the actions. The instructions are chosen by students from the Instruction Book.

> **Higher levels**
> You could let students add extra commands to the instructions.
> e.g. *Walk up the wall. Come back. Turn in a circle.*

Note: *Do-it-yourself* decorating is one of the most popular leisure activities in Britain.

Before you watch

1 Can you remember? Which things can you see in section four?

Students shouldn't tick the boxes at this point – this comes in *While you watch* below. They can compare their knowledge in pairs, or you could take a class vote before *While you watch*. However, you shouldn't reveal whether their answers are correct at this point.

Answers
the inside of Gromit's old room
the inside of Gromit's new room ✔
the living-room ✔
the bathroom door ✔
the inside of the bathroom
the door of Gromit's old room ✔
the back yard ✔
the window of Gromit's old room ✔
Gromit's kennel ✔

While you watch

2 What can you see in section 4?
Tick (✔) the places in exercise 1.

Watch section four.

After you watch

3 Ask and answer these questions.

Have students ask and answer questions in pairs. Check by asking individuals selected at random. The short answer is the natural one here. We would not insist on *No, Gromit can't sleep*.

Answers
1 The music's very loud. Can Gromit sleep?
   No, he can't.
2 Gromit is downstairs on the sofa. Is the penguin upstairs?
   No, he isn't.
3 Gromit knocks on the door. Is the penguin inside?
   No, he isn't.
4 Gromit can hear the music outside. Is the penguin in his room?
   No, he isn't.
5 The penguin's home. Can Gromit still hear the music?
   No, he can't.

Note: The first piece of organ music in this section is *Happy Talk* from the musical *South Pacific*.

The second piece of organ music, when Gromit is outside, is a 1950's novelty song called *How much is that doggie in the window?* Again, this is of no importance, but it is irritating when you can't remember.

Watch all of episode two again.

Exercises

1 Memory
Are these sentences true (✔) or false (✘)?
Answers
1 Wallace can't program the techno-trousers. ✘
2 The techno-trousers are ex-NASA. ✔
3 The toy dog is on wheels. ✘
4 Penguins don't like fish. ✘
5 The spare room is seventy pounds a week. ✘
6 The spare room isn't dark. ✘
7 The important rule is 'No pets.' ✔
8 Gromit's favourite wallpaper is red. ✘
9 Gromit's kennel is inside. ✘

Now correct the false sentences.
Answers
1 Wallace can program the techno-trousers.
4 Penguins like fish,
5 The spare room is twenty pounds a week.
6 The spare room is dark.
8 Gromit's favourite wallpaper is blue / blue and white.
9 Gromit's kennel is outside.

2 Test yourself
Choose the correct word in (brackets).
Answers
1 You (can / can't) see your birthday present now.
2 How (are / is) the techno-trousers?
3 There (are / is) someone at the door.
4 What (do / would) you like for breakfast?
5 It's a nice big room, and (it's / it) very cheap.
6 (Don't / Do not) worry, Gromit.
7 (You / You've) got your favourite wallpaper.
8 And he can (here / hear) it downstairs.
9 He can hear the music outside (two / too).

Now check with the Transcript on page 23.
It's much more valuable to encourage students to check for themselves. This encourages speed-reading and skimming skills. They can do this in co-operation with a partner. Don't give corrections until they have had time to self-check.

3 Contractions of *is* or *has*
Gromit's on wheels = Gromit is on wheels.
Gromit's got the instruction book = Gromit has got the instruction book.

Does *'s* mean *is* or *has* in these sentences?
Answers
1 Where's your lead? – is
2 Gromit's got his favourite wallpaper. – has
3 Wallace's got a spare room. – has
4 It's this way. – is

4 Sounds
Say these words aloud:
no / on

o has got two different sounds here.

Put these words in the correct sound group: A or B.
collar / dog / show / so / follow / follow / got / toast / drop / owner / sorry / knock / post / problem / cold

Encourage students to say the words 'aloud in their heads' while doing this exercise. It should be checked orally.

Answers
A (no)
show / so / toast / owner / post / follow / cold

B (on)
collar / dog / got / drop / sorry / knock / problem / follow

Transfer

1 Likes and dislikes
Gromit likes knitting. Gromit likes darts.

Knitting and darts are both illustrated. The rest should be known or guessable. Remember that you can explain words like *swimming* and *playing tennis* by miming the actions.

food and drink	music	hobbies
toast	pop music	dancing
pizza	classical music	football
spaghetti	rap music	video games
burgers	organ music	knitting
tea	rock and roll	darts
coffee	jazz	swimming
milk	folk music	walking
cola	dance music	tennis
lemonade	film soundtracks	watching TV

Look at the words above. Make a list. Write four sentences about you with *I like …* and four sentences with *I don't like …*
Students will choose only eight items, but they should answer truthfully for all the questions. The questioner should check *Is it on your list?* for each one.

Ask your partner about his / her list.

● *Do you like toast?*
■ *Yes, I do. / No, I don't.*

While doing this, it is useful to mark their partners answers on the list in preparation for 2 when they change partners.

2 Change partners. Ask and answer questions about your first partner.

● *Does she like tea?*
■ *Yes, she does. / No, she doesn't.*

If they have marked their list with their partner's answers, they should be able to answer accurately for all of them. When the activity has been completed, ask a few questions around the room in a conversational way.

e.g.
Do you like playing tennis, Paul?
Does Maria like playing tennis, Anna?
What does Maria like, Anna?

Then get students to ask you about your likes and dislikes. They will find this much more interesting! You can choose whether to answer truthfully or not.

> **Higher levels**
> **Take the opportunity of adding currently popular things into the question and answer above:** *Do you like …* **(a current TV programme / a film / a book / a rock group / a fashion item)? You could also ask question generators.**
>
> **e.g.**
> *T: Paul, do you like spaghetti?*
> *Student 1: Yes, I do.*
> *T: Ask Maria, 'burgers'*
> *Student 1: Do you like burgers, Maria?*
> *Student 2: No, I don't.*
> *T: (indicates S3): Ask her, 'What?'*
> *Student 3: What do you like, Maria?*
> *Student 2: I like pizza.*

> See: Grammar page 22, 2 Likes and dislikes

3 In your bedroom

They should mark their partner's answers as before in preparation for changing partners.

TV	alarm clock	dictionary
picture	cassette player	desk
chair	mirror	computer

Look at the words above. Ask and answer questions.

● *Have you got a TV in your bedroom?*
■ *Yes, I have. / No, I haven't.*

You can ask about things in the picture on page 20 too.

4 Change partners. Ask and answer questions about your first partner.

● *Has she got a mirror in her room?*
■ *Yes, she has. / No, she hasn't.*

As above, finish this by asking questions around the class in a conversational way.

e.g.
T: Have you got a chair in your room?
Student 1: Yes, I have.
T: Ask Paul.
Student 1: Have you got a chair in your room, Paul?
Student 2: No, I haven't.
T: (indicates S3) Ask me.
Student 3: Have you got a chair in your room?
T: No, I haven't …

Remember that they will enjoy asking you more than they will each other.

Warning: This activity has the potential for revealing differences in wealth. You may wish to avoid this in some classes.

Note: More British children have televisions in their own rooms than any other nationality (including the USA). However, televisions are comparatively cheap in Britain.

> **Higher levels**
> **If vocabulary is no problem, the practice could be extended to other rooms in the house.**

> See: Vocabulary, page 20, 1 Gromit's room
> and Grammar, page 12, 3 *have got / has got*

5 What can you do? Ask and answer questions.

Students should mark their partner's answers as before in preparation for changing partners.

● *Can you knit?*
■ *Yes, I can. / No, I can't.*

Use these words.

knit / cook / drive / play darts / speak English / dance / ride a bicycle / sing

6 Change partners. Ask and answer questions about your first partner.

● *Can she knit?*
■ *Yes, she can. / No, she can't.*

Just as in the two previous sections, move into conversational questions around the class. Try and keep this informal, as if you are asking out of genuine interest.

e.g.
T: Can you knit, Anna?
Student 1: No, I can't.
T: Hmm. Ask Paul.
Student 1: Can you knit, Paul?
Student 2: Yes, I can.
T: (indicate S3) Ask me.
Student 3: Can you knit?

Don't forget that they will enjoy asking you about your abilities, so encourage them to do this.

See: Grammar, page 22, 1 *can, can't*

Vocabulary

1 Gromit's room
Read this. Look at the bold words. Put them in the correct boxes on the picture.

This is Gromit's bedroom. The penguin's sitting on Gromit's bed. There's a yellow **bedspread** on the bed. There's a **bedside cabinet** beside the bed. There's a **radio** and an **alarm-clock** on the cabinet. There's a **tennis racket** beside it. There are some **bookshelves** on the other side of the bed. There's a small **bedside lamp** on the bookshelves. There's a small **bookshelf** on the wall in the top left of the picture. Gromit has got an old brown **chest of drawers** and there's a **model ship** on the top. There's a yellow Batman **kite** in the corner of the room. On the floor, there's a **toy helicopter**, an orange **toy robot** and there's a **record player** and some records. On the wall above the bed is Gromit's favourite **picture**. It's a picture of a bone. There are pictures of bones on the wallpaper too.

Students should work individually then compare in pairs. Check with the class.

Answers (begin at the top left corner and go round clockwise)
bookshelf / picture / bedside lamp / bookshelves / kite / model ship / chest of drawers / robot / toy helicopter / bedspread / bedside cabinet / record player / tennis racket / radio / alarm clock

2 Bed + room
Bed + room → bedroom.

Match words from Box 1 with words from Box 2.

Box 1				
step	book	paint	wall	bed

Box 2				
paper	brush	ladder	shelves	spread

Answers
stepladder / bookshelves / paintbrush / wallpaper / bedspread

3 Decorating
Put the words under the correct pictures.

Answers (from top to bottom, then left to right)
paintbrush
stepladder
hammer
roller
screwdriver
electric drill
tin of paint
roll of wallpaper
ladder

4 Vocabulary notebook
Write translations. You can use your dictionary.

In most cases students will gain great advantage by using a monolingual dictionary with simplified English explanations. However, at this level a bilingual dictionary is the best for this exercise. You may wish to check that the correct translations are given for the word in its context in the episode.

You may wish to write in model translations here for reference.

again	----------	outside	-------------
big	----------	paint	-------------
book	----------	pay	-------------
ceiling	----------	pet	-------------
cold	----------	poor	-------------
dark	----------	program	-------------
decorate	----------	quiet	-------------
door	----------	rule	-------------
down	----------	see	-------------
downstairs	----------	show	-------------
fantastic	----------	slide	-------------
favourite	----------	spare	-------------
fish	----------	suction	-------------
forward	----------	toy	-------------
important	----------	trousers	-------------
instruction	----------	try	-------------
knock	----------	upside down	-------------
leg	----------	walk	-------------
loud	----------	walkies	-------------
minutes	----------	wall	-------------
music	----------	wallpaper	-------------

Grammar

See: Student's Book, page 22

You may wish to spend time going through this. If so, we would encourage activating the student's language by introducing drills, questions, etc.

Transcript

See: Student's Book, page 23

Episode 3

Wallace, Gromit & the penguin!

Watching the video

To the teacher: This episode has only three sections.

The structures here are the Present continuous and *going to* for future use. These lend themselves to exploitation where the teacher freezes the tape and says *What's happening now?* or *What's going to happen next?*

> **Higher levels**
> You could view the whole episode with the TV sound off, then pausing the tape to ask *What's (he) doing now?* or *What's going to happen next?* at intervals. This would either precede or replace page 24.

Before you watch

1 Complete the sentences with words from the box.

The Present continuous hasn't appeared in the episodes so far, but even student's who are unfamiliar with the structure should be able to do this without much help. Don't get involved in any lengthy explanation at this point.

sleeping	feeling	wearing

Answers

Poor Gromit! He's outside in his kennel. It's a cold night. He's wearing ear-muffs and he's got a blanket. The penguin has got Gromit's room. And he's sleeping in Gromit's bed. Gromit's feeling very sad. He's going to cry.

Watch all of episode three.

After you watch

2 Can you remember?

We suggest having students do this in pairs first. Then check by asking the questions to individuals selected at random. You can decide whether you want complete sentences (as in the answers below) or whether you will accept single words.

Answers

1 The penguin's holding the slippers. What's Wallace holding?
   He's holding a hair-dryer.

2 Who's going to get the newspaper?
   The penguin's going to get the newspaper.

3 What's inside the red and white handkerchief?
   There's a brush, a bone and an alarm clock (inside the handkerchief).

4 What is the title of the book?
   The title is *Electronics for Dogs*.

5 The penguin's holding a book and a drill. What's the penguin looking at?
   The penguin's looking at the techno-trousers.

SECTION ONE	**00.00 to 00.52**

Before you watch

1 Complete the sentences with words from the box.

going to	holding	can't	cleaning	standing

Answers

Gromit is standing outside the bathroom. He's holding his towel. It's light green. He's going to have a wash. He can't have a wash now, because the penguin's in the bathroom. The penguin's cleaning his teeth.

Note: You could ask *Have penguins got teeth?* With better classes you could suggest *The penguin's cleaning his beak* as an alternative. For some reason, English speakers seem more or less equally divided in preference for *cleaning teeth* and *brushing teeth*.

Watch section one.

After you watch

2 Answer the questions.

Answers

1 Is he reading a book, or is he watching television?
   He's reading a book.

2 Is he drying his hair, or is he drying his ears?
   You can invite suggestions here – normally we dry our hair, but Wallace hasn't got any, and his ears are moving! Accept both as correct and make a joke of it.

3 Is Gromit going to get the newspaper, or is the penguin going to get the newspaper?
   The penguin's going to get the newspaper.

4 Is Gromit growling at Wallace, or is he growling at the penguin?
   Gromit's growling at the penguin.

3 Question words
Look at the questions in 2 above. Put *What* or *Who* in the spaces below.

1 What is Gromit doing?
2 What is Wallace drying?
3 Who is going to get the newspaper?
4 Who is Gromit growling at?

> See: Grammar, page 32, 1 Present continuous, 2 *going to* future

We would prefer to finish the episode before going into a formal grammar explanation, but you may wish to refer to *Grammar* at this point.

Notes:
1 *That's just grand – grand* is a regionalism meaning very good.

2 While we don't suggest explaining all the visual jokes, note that Gromit is reading *The Republic* by Pluto. *The Republic* was by the philosopher Plato. Pluto is the Walt Disney dog.

SECTION TWO	00.52 to 01.36

Higher levels
You could do silent viewing, pausing to ask *What's he doing? What's he going to do?*

While you watch

1 You're going to see these things in section two. Number the sentences from 1 to 5.

Gromit is putting his favourite things
   into a handkerchief. – 3
Wallace and the penguin are having dinner. – 2
There are tears in Gromit's eyes. – 5
Gromit is looking at a photograph. – 4
There is the first flash of lightning. – 1

You could explain: *You hear thunder. You see lightning. There's going to be a thunderstorm./ It's going to thunder.*

Watch section two.

After you watch

2 What are they doing? Ask and answer the questions below.

Students ask and answer questions in pairs.

Answers
1 Who is Gromit watching?
   Gromit / He's watching Wallace and the penguin.

2 What are they eating?
   They're eating cheese.

3 What are they drinking?
   They're drinking wine / champagne / water.
   (They're drinking from glasses, so it's a cold drink.)

4 Are they enjoying their dinner?
   Yes, they are.

3 Look at the picture. What's Gromit going to do?

Ask and answer these questions.

Answers:
1 What's he going to put into the handkerchief?
   He's going to put a bone, a brush and an alarm clock into the handkerchief.

2 Is he going to take a book with him?
   No, he isn't.

3 Is he going to take the photograph with him?
   No, he isn't.

4 Is he going to switch off the light?
   Yes, he is.

You could ask students to spot the titles of the books – 'Sticks', 'Sheep II', 'Bones'. You would have to explain these items.

Higher levels
Ask them to describe the inside of Gromit's kennel.
e.g.
It's got wallpaper / his favourite wallpaper. It's got an electric light. There's a bookshelf with books. There's a photograph in a frame. There's a bone on a shelf.

SECTION THREE	01.36 to 02.25

Before you watch

1 Ask and answer these questions.

Answers
1 Is Gromit feeling sad and lonely?
   Yes, he is.

2 Are you feeling sad about Gromit?
   Free answer: Yes, I am. / No, I'm not.

3 Do you like the penguin?
   Free answer: Yes, I do. / No, I don't.

4 Do you like stories with a happy ending?
   Free answer: Yes, I do. / No, I don't.

5 Have you got tears in your eyes?
   Free answer: Yes, I have. / No, I haven't.

Watch section three.

After you watch

2 Are these sentences true (✔) or false (✘)?

1 The penguin is watching Gromit. ✔
2 The penguin is feeling sad. ✘
3 The penguin has got a plan. ✔

3 What's the penguin going to do? Choose one answer.

He's going to put a picture on the wall.
He's going to change the electronics on the techno-trousers.
He's going to make a present for Wallace.

Answer
The correct answer is 2, but students have no way of knowing this at this point. Don't correct – leave it as their opinion.

Before you watch episode three again

1 You are going to watch episode three again. What's going to happen? Make sentences. e.g.

penguin / get Wallace's slippers
The penguin's going to get Wallace's slippers.

Answers
1 Gromit / not / get the newspaper
Gromit isn't going to get the newspaper.

2 penguin / get the newspaper
The penguin's going to get the newspaper.

3 Gromit / eat cornflakes
Gromit's going to eat cornflakes / some cornflakes.

4 Gromit / not / have dinner with Wallace and the penguin
Gromit isn't going to have dinner with Wallace and the penguin.

5 Gromit / leave home
Gromit's going to leave home.

> **Higher levels**
> Note: *leave home*, there is no article (*not leave the home*).

5 Make three more sentences with *going to* (*do*).

This is a free activity.

e.g.
Gromit's going to read a book.
The penguin's going to get the slippers for Wallace / Wallace's slippers.
Gromit's going to wait for the bathroom.
It's going to thunder.
Gromit's going to put his favourite things in the handkerchief.
Gromit's going to cry.

Get the class as a whole to give ideas. You could list the possibilities on the board.

Watch all of episode three again.

> **Higher levels**
> If you didn't do silent viewing, pausing to ask questions, earlier, then you could do it at this point.

Exercises

1 Memory
Are these sentences true (✔) or false (✗)?

Answers
1 Gromit's towel is dark green. ✗
2 Wallace's hair-dryer is pink. ✔
3 Wallace is holding a brown mirror. ✔
4 Gromit is reading 'The Republic' by Plato. ✗
5 The television is brown and black. ✗
6 There isn't an electric light in Gromit's kennel. ✗
7 We see five book titles: 'The Republic', 'Bones', 'Sticks', 'Sheep II' and 'Electronics for Dogs'. ✔

Now correct the false sentences.

Answers
1 Gromit's towel is light green.
4 Gromit is reading 'The Republic' by Pluto.
5 The television is white and black.
6 There is an electric light in Gromit's kennel.

> **Higher levels**
> Check that the students stress the altered words – those in bold above – when saying the corrected sentences.

2 Test yourself
Choose the correct word in (brackets).

Answers
1 (Who's / Whose) in the bathroom, Gromit?
2 You're (slowly / slow) this morning, Gromit.
3 Well (doing / done), Penguin! Cheers!
4 Enjoy (your / yours) dinner, Penguin!
5 Goodnight, Penguin. Sleep (well / good)!
6 (Some / More) cheese, Penguin?
7 They're (have / having) fun.

Now check with the Transcript on page 33.

Have students self-check before you give the correct answers.

3 Negatives
Make these sentences negative. e.g.

He's waiting for the bathroom.

He isn't waiting for the bathroom.

Answers
1 I'm reading.
I'm not reading.
2 You're writing.
You aren't writing.
3 It's raining.
It isn't raining.
4 She's sleeping.
She isn't sleeping.
5 We're watching the video.
We aren't watching the video.
6 They're having breakfast.
They aren't having breakfast.

This could be preceded (or followed) by the same exercise done as an oral drill. First with the class in chorus, then selecting individuals at random.

Higher levels
Introduce a progressive substitution drill.
e.g.
T: I'm not reading.
Student: I'm not reading.
T: They
Student: They aren't reading.
Continue: She / is / sleeping / We / aren't / listening / You / I / not

Having done it chorally, repeat the drill, selecting individuals to respond at random.

4 Questions
Make the sentences in exercise 3 into questions.
e.g.

He's waiting for the bathroom.

Is he waiting for the bathroom?

Answers
Am I reading?
Are you writing?
Is it raining?
Is she sleeping?
Are we watching the video?
Are they having breakfast?

Again, this could be done orally either before or after doing it in writing.

Higher levels
The exercise could become another progressive substitution drill.
e.g.
T: Is he waiting for the bathroom?
Student: Is he waiting for the bathroom?
T: they
Student: Are they waiting for the bathroom?
Continue: train / she / you / bus / we / plane / he

See: Grammar, page 32, 1 Present continuous

5 Sounds
Say these words aloud:
have, alarm, rain

Look at the red vowels. Put these words from episodes 1 to 3 in the correct sound group: A, B or C.

bathroom	carrying	newspaper	late
that	pain	back	card
date	jam	safe	again
favourite	dark	paint	pay

Answers
A (have)
carrying / that / back / jam
B (alarm)
bathroom / card / dark
C (rain)
newspaper / late / pain / date / safe / again / favourite / paint / pay

Higher levels
You can choose whether to introduce phonetics with this exercise.

Transfer

1 What have you got in your wardrobe?
Look at the pictures and ask a partner.

Students work in pairs. Encourage them to note their partner's answers.

dress / skirt / jacket / blouse / jeans / coat / trainers / T-shirt

● *Have you got a white T-shirt?*
■ *Yes, I have.*
● *Have you got any brown shoes?*
■ *No, I haven't.*

Higher levels
Students could change partners and ask and answer questions about their previous partner: *Has (she) got a white T-shirt? Has she got (pink) trainers?* etc.

See also: Vocabulary, page 30, 1 and 2 Clothes

2 What is she wearing?
Ask and answer questions about people in your class.

Students work in pairs.

● *What's (Anna) wearing?*
■ *She's wearing a blue skirt, and a red and white striped blouse.*
● *Who's wearing blue jeans and a light blue shirt?*
■ *(Mark) is wearing blue jeans and a light blue shirt.*

After the pairwork, ask questions in a conversational manner to check. This is a good point for widening vocabulary to include items not illustrated in the unit. It's important to describe what is in the room. Also ask *What am I wearing?* so students can describe your clothes. Add adjectives. If a student says *You're wearing a white (blouse).* Change it to *I'm wearing a beautiful white blouse*, or *I'm wearing a new white blouse*, (or *a nice white blouse, an expensive white blouse*, etc),

See: Grammar, page 32, 1 Present continuous

3 What are you going to do?
Write your plans for next week in the diary.
e.g.

Monday – play tennis

Note: *stay at home* is the most likely answer for students in most places. If so, you can ask *What are you going to do at home?* etc. There is a tendency for textbooks to assume that everyone is going to do seven different interesting things over the next week which is unlikely. Students work individually. Circulate and give help. This may be stretching their vocabulary. You could suggest things by asking questions to individuals.

e.g.
Are you going dancing? Are you going to watch a film? Are you going to meet your friends? Are you going to see some relatives? Are you going to go to a restaurant? Are you going to play football? etc.

The pairwork is based on the diaries.

Ask and answer questions.

● *What are you going to do on Monday?*
■ *I'm going to play tennis.*

Then ask:

● *When are you going to play tennis?*
■ *I'm going to play tennis on Monday.*

4 Change partners.
Ask and answer questions about your first partner.

● *What is she going to do on Monday?*
■ *She's going to play tennis.*

Check by asking the class similar questions. Modify the questions to introduce other topics / plans. Have students ask you about your plans. We think it's worth preparing an interesting and exciting set of plans!

> **Higher levels**
> **Introduce question generators and additional questions.**
> **e.g.**
> *T: When are you going to watch a film?*
> *Student 1: I'm going to watch a film on Saturday.*
> *T: (indicate S2) Ask 'Which film?'*
> *Student 2: Which film are you going to see?*
> *Student 1: I'm going to see 'Titanic.'*
> *T: What are you going to do on Friday, Paul?*
> *Student 3: I'm going to stay at home.*
> *T: What are you going to do at home?*
> *Student 3: I'm going to play computer games.*
> *T: Who are you going to play with?*
> *Student 3: I'm going to play with my sister.*
> *T: Does she like computer games? / Has she got a computer? etc.*
>
> **When students start to get interested, do not try and stick solely to the target structure!**

See: Grammar, page 32, 2 *going to* future

Vocabulary

1 Clothes (1)

Wallace is wearing a **plain** red **dressing gown** and blue and white **striped pyjamas**. He's wearing **tartan slippers**.

Wallace is wearing a **plain** green **sleeveless pullover**, a white **shirt** and a red **tie**. He's wearing **plain** brown **trousers**. He's still wearing the tartan slippers.

Gromit's wearing a yellow **mac** and a yellow **rain hat**. He's carrying his favourite things in a red and white **spotted handkerchief**.

Label these pictures, e.g. *brown and yellow striped*.

Answers (from left to right)
grey and black striped
plain pink
blue and white spotted
red and green tartan
brown and yellow striped

2 Clothes (2)
How many words can you put on the chart below?

This is a free activity. Some suggestions have been put on the chart. You should encourage students to add things which can be seen in the classroom.

clothes above the waist	clothes below the waist	on the feet	around the neck	above and below the waist
shirt	trousers	shoes	tie	dress
blouse	jeans	boots	scarf	suit
jacket	tights	socks	necklace	overcoat / coat
T-shirt	leggings	pop socks		raincoat / mac
pullover		trainers		pyjamas
hat		slippers		dressing-gown

3 *have (breakfast)*
Look at these sentences.

Gromit's having breakfast.
He's having cornflakes for breakfast.
He's going to have a wash.
Wallace and the penguin are having dinner.
They're having fun.

Note some words we use with *have*.

have			
breakfast	lunch	dinner	coffee
a holiday	fun	a rest	an idea

> **Higher levels**
> **Ask students to make sample sentences.**

See also: Transfer, page 29, 1 What have you got in your wardrobe?

4 The weather

(be) cloudy

rain

snow

thunder

(be) windy

(be) sunny

Note: We say 'It's going to *thunder*', but *thunder* is the noise, and we see *lightning*.

Ask and answer questions about next week's weather.

● *Is it going to rain?*
■ *Yes, it is. / No, it isn't.*
● *Is it going to be cloudy?*
■ *Yes, it is. / No, it isn't.*

Students ask and answer in pairs. Check with the class as a whole. You could add a drill.

e.g.
T: Rain.
Student: Is it going to rain?

Continue: thunder / snow / be sunny / be cloudy / be windy

Repeat with individuals selected at random after the choral drill.

5 Vocabulary notebook
Write translations. You can use your dictionary.

In most cases students will gain great advantage by using a monolingual dictionary with simplified English explanations. However, at this level a bilingual dictionary is the best for this exercise. You may wish to check that the correct translations are given for the word in its context in the episode.

You may wish to write in model translations here for reference.

alarm clock	----------	kennel	---------
bathroom	----------	late	---------
best	----------	leave	---------
blanket	----------	mirror	---------
bone	----------	newspaper	---------
brush	----------	pair	---------
carry	----------	put on	---------
cheers	----------	pyjamas	---------
cheese	----------	rain	---------
dressing-gown	----------	slippers	---------
drill	----------	slow	---------
ear-muffs	----------	spotted	---------
electric	----------	striped	---------
electronics	----------	switch off	---------
friends	----------	switch on	---------
fun	----------	tartan	---------
grand	----------	tears	---------
hair-dryer	----------	thunder	---------
handkerchief	----------	wear	---------
hold	----------	well	---------
home	----------		

Grammar

See: Student's Book, page 32

You may wish to spend time going through this. If so, we would encourage activating the student's language by introducing drills, questions, etc.

Transcript

See: Student's Book, page 33

Episode 4

The penguin's plan

Watching the video

Before you watch

This episode introduces *was* and *were* for the past tense. This gives you the opportunity to ask about the earlier episodes.

1 Where were Wallace and Gromit in episodes one to three? Tick (✔) the correct answers.

Wallace was in the kitchen.
Wallace was upstairs in bed.✔

Wallace was on the stairs. ✔
Wallace was at the front door.

Wallace was in the chair. ✔
Wallace was at the table.

Gromit was on the slide. ✔
Gromit was at home.

Gromit was on the ladder.
Gromit was on the ceiling. ✔

Gromit was in his kennel. ✔
Gromit was in the street.

Have students work individually. Check by asking questions.

e.g.
Picture 1: Was Wallis in the kitchen? Was he downstairs or was he upstairs? Where was he?
Picture 2: Was Wallis at the front door? Where was he?
Picture 3: Was Wallace at the table? Where was he?
Picture 4: Was Gromit at home? Where was he?
Picture 5: Was Gromit on the ladder? Who was on the ladder? Where was Gromit?
Picture 6: Was Gromit in the house? Was he in the street? Where was he? Where was Wallace? Where was the penguin?

> **Higher levels**
> **Modify and extend the question sequence above. Elicit a negative answer, then use a question generator.**
> **e.g.**
> *T: Was Wallis in the kitchen?*
> *Student 1: No, he wasn't.*
> *T: (indicates Student 2) Ask 'Where?'*
> *Student 2: Where was he?*
> *T: (indicates Student 3)*
> *Student 3: He was upstairs in bed.*
> *T: (indicates Student 4) Was Gromit upstairs?*
> *Student 4: No, he wasn't.*
> *T: (indicates Student 5) Ask 'Where?'*
> *Student 5: Where was Gromit?*
> *T: (indicates Student 6)*
> *Student 6: Gromit was downstairs.*

Watch all of episode four.

After you watch

2 Storyboard. Look at the scenes. Put the words under the correct pictures.

a shop	window	the living-room
the penguin's room	a café	a builder's yard

When you check back, you could subtlely use more examples of *was/were* by asking questions.

e.g.
Look at number three. Where was Wallace?
Was he in the bedroom? Was he in the kitchen? etc.

Answers
1   under a bridge
2   Wallace'sbedroom
3   the living-room
4   West Wallaby Street
5   a shop window
6   a builder's yard
7   Wallace's bedroom
8   a café
9   a street by some tall buildings
10 the door
11 the penguin's room
12 Wallace's bedroom

Note: The story starts under a bridge. The dustbins (American English: *trash cans*) are classic cartoon dustbins, and this image of a dustbin is still used on computers for 'trash'. However, in Britain they have long since been replaced by plastic wheelie-bins (larger dustbins on wheels).

SECTION ONE	**00.00 to 00.57**

Before you watch

1 Find Wallace and Gromit. Put arrows (→) on the pictures.

This is rather like the 'Spot the (foot)ball' competition in newspapers. If these are popular, ask students about them. Students should make their choices, then compare with a partner in pairs. You can then decide who is nearest the exact position, replaying the tape if necessary.

Watch section one.

After you watch

2 Look at the pictures again.

Students answer individually.

Answers
1   Are your arrows in the correct places?
    Yes, they are. / No, they aren't.
2   Are your partner's arrows in the correct places?
    Yes, they are. / No, they aren't.
3   Who is inside the dustbin?
    Gromit's inside the dustbin.
4   Is Wallace above the roof or behind the roof?
    Wallace is behind the roof (Note: You can just see Wallace's hands behind the roof).

Check back with the class. Ask questions:

e.g.
Were you correct? Was your partner correct?

3 Ask and answer these questions about the techno-trousers.

Students work in pairs. It is your choice whether to accept short answers or full sentences for 2 and 3.

Answers
1 Who's wearing them?
   Wallace is wearing them.
2 Has Gromit got the controls?
   No, he hasn't. / No, he hasn't got the controls.
3 Can Wallace stop them?
   No, he can't. / No, Wallace can't stop them.

Check back with the class.

SECTION TWO   **00.58 to 02.31**

Before you watch

1 What's wrong with these notices? Correct them.

Note: Newsagents and other shops often have 'small ads' on postcards. You can compare *Apply within* with its earlier occurence in episode 2. Here it means that you ask in the shop. *Reasonable* means 'not very much' in this sense. The terms are the conditions – the price and the rules. 'No dogs' and 'No pets' are common in this sort of advert.

Answers
ROOM TO LET   POLICE NOTICE
REASONABLE TERMS   WANTED
NO DOGS!   HAVE YOU SEEN THIS
APPLY WITHIN   CHICKEN?
                £1000 REWARD

Watch section two and check.

Pause the video at the notices and allow students to self-check.

Warning: The Present perfect is not part of the syllabus of this course. However, it is on the notice. Try to avoid explanation, treating it as a fixed formula, but if you can't, explain as briefly as possible. This means 'in your life until now'.

> **Higher levels**
> You could briefly extend practice on *Have you seen...?* while still treating it as a formula rather than a structure. You could ask about films and TV programmes, restricting it absolutely to *seen*. If they are confident with this, it would be possible to add *been* (*Have you ever been to England?*). They should be able to deal with simple manipulation into 3rd person, as they know *has/have got*. e.g, *Has (your partner) ever seen 'Titanic'?*
> However, it would be easy to get lost in this at the expense of continuing the story!

After you watch

2 Choose the correct answers.

Students work individually and compare in pairs. When you check through, you can add the explanations annotated below.

Answers
1 Gromit is looking for a room. There's an advert for a room in the shop window. Why can't Gromit rent it?
   The room is very expensive.
   The rule is 'No dogs.' ✔
   If it's reasonable terms it means it is not expensive.

2 There's a police 'Wanted' poster. What can you see on the poster?
   a chicken
   a penguin with a funny hat ✔

We would be careful about answering this – it is of course the penguin with a funny hat, but Gromit has not yet realised this. You might want to leave it open.

3 Gromit is looking at the poster. What is he thinking?
   I know that chicken. I'm sure.
   Do I know that chicken? I'm not sure. ✔

We don't think Gromit is sure … but there is a degree of opinion in this.

4 Wallace is in the wrong trousers. Who is controlling them?
   The penguin. ✔
   Gromit.

SECTION THREE   **02.32 to 04.36**

Before you watch

Note: Exercise 2 is to the right of exercise 1. Exercise 3 is below it.

In this section students are asked questions which involve new vocabulary without pre-teaching the words (i.e. Don't ask what *window-ledge* means.). They should be encouraged to guess from the pictures.

1 Label the pictures with these words.

penknife / cardboard box / tape measure / notebook

Students work alone. Check quickly.

Answers (from left to right)

penknife / notebook / cardboard box / tape measure

2 What can you do?
Look at the pictures and complete the sentences with these words.

hide / write / cut / measure

1 You can measure things with a tape measure.
2 You can cut things with a penknife.
3 You can write in a notebook.
4 You can hide in a cardboard box.

Check by asking questions, e.g. *What can you do with a penknife?* etc.

Watch section three.

After you watch

3 Where's Gromit hiding?
Ask and answer questions about the pictures.
You can use these words.

in	the corner of a building
behind	the dustbins
round	the newspaper
	the cardboard box

Students ask and answer questions in pairs.

Model answers
He's hiding behind a newspaper.
He's hiding round the corner of a building.
He's hiding behind the dustbins.
He's hiding in the cardboard box.

4 Ask and answer these questions.

Students ask and answer questions in pairs.

Note: Don't explain the word order, but gently correct if students say *how wide is the window*.

Answers
1 Where's the penguin standing, in the street or on the window ledge?
The penguin's standing on the window ledge.

2 Is he measuring how wide the window is, or how high the window is?
He's measuring how wide the window is.

3 Is Gromit looking through a hole in the box, or through a hole in the dustbin?
Gromit's looking through a hole in the box.

5 Say these words aloud:

1 Watch out!   2 Be careful, Gromit!   3 Uh oh!

Have students do this chorally and individually, paying attention to being expressive. Don't allow monotonous delivery.

Watch section three without sound.

6 Work in pairs. Watch section three again without sound.

Student A closes her / his eyes. Student B describes what is happening.

Then watch section three a third time. Student B closes her / his eyes. Student A describes what is happening.

This is a free activity where students have the chance to explore what they can say. Correction should be avoided. You may wish to encourage them to use the Present continuous, but they should be allowed to use whatever language they can.

> **Higher levels**
> **This activity is suitable for many video sequences.**
> **You can be more targeted at higher levels, and if students can cope, we would try to get them to do this using the Present continuous as far as possible.**

Before you watch

1 What's Gromit doing? Ask and answer these questions.

Students ask and answer questions in pairs. Check with the class.

Answers
1 Where is Gromit?
He's in the penguin's room.
2 What's he looking at?
He's looking at the plans (of the City Museum).
3 Where is Gromit?
He's in Wallace's bed / He's under the bedspread.
4 Who's he looking at?
He's looking at the penguin.

Watch section four.

After you watch

2 Complete the sentences with words from the box.

Students work alone then compare answers in pairs. Check with the class.

e.g.

It was your room. It's the penguin's room now.

| is | isn't | are | aren't | was | were |

Answers
1 The wallpaper in Gromit's room was blue, but now it is / 's yellow.
2 There were bones on the wallpaper, but now there are fish.
3 The bones were white, but the fish are pink.
4 In episode three, there was a dog flap in the door. It isn't / is not there now. There is / is not / 's a penguin flap in the door now.
5 The dog flap was grey, but the penguin flap is red.
6 The controls were on the trousers in episode two, but they aren't on the trousers now. The penguin's got them.
7 Gromit was in the trousers in episode two, but Wallace is / 's in the trousers now.

When you check back, ask questions.

e.g.

What colour is the wallpaper now? What colour was the wallpaper before?

Were there fish on the wallpaper before? Are there fish on the wallpaper now?

What colour are the fish? What colour were the bones?

What was in the door in epoisode 3? Is it there now? What is there now?

What colour was the dog flap? What colour is the penguin flap?

Were the controls on the trousers in episode 2? Are they on the trousers now? Who has got them?

Who was in the trousers in episode 2? Who is in the trousers now?

See: Grammar, page 42, 1 *was, were*

Watch all of episode four again.

Exercises

1 Memory
Are these sentences true (✔) or false (✗)?

Answers
1 Wallace is wearing a string vest. ✔
2 Wallace can control the trousers. ✗
3 There are two bottles of milk outside Wallace's front door. ✔
4 There's a picture of toast and jam above Wallace's bed. ✗
5 The tablecloths in the café are blue and white. ✗
6 The diamond exhibition is at the café. ✗
7 There are slippers on Wallace's bed. ✔
8 Gromit is hiding under the bedspread. ✔

Now correct the false sentences.

Answers
2 Wallace can't control the trousers.
4 There's a picture of cheese above Wallace's bed.
5 The tablecloths in the café are red and white.
6 The diamond exhibition is at the City Museum.

2 Test yourself
Choose the correct word in (brackets).

Answers
1 That (were / was) lovely cheese.
2 Wait (a / the) minute!
3 Help me! I can't stop (it / them).
4 I'm going to sleep in (my / me) lovely bed.
5 He's writing (someone / something).
6 (Keep / Be) careful, Gromit!
7 He's (measuring / measure) the window.
8 (No one's / Nothing) here.

Now check with the Transcript on page 43.

Have students self-check before you give the correct answers.

3 Make sentences.

Look at Gromit.
Look at him.

Continue. Use these words:

it / us / her / him / them

Answers
1 Look at Mrs Grant.
   Look at her.
2 Look at Wallace.
   Look at him.
3 Look at John and me.
   Look at us.
4 Look at Mr and Mrs Smith.
   Look at them.
5 Look at the book.
   Look at it.

See: Grammar, page 42, 2 Object pronouns

Refer to the Grammar section if necessary. Check by repeating the exercise as an oral drill with books closed.

4 Sounds
Say these words aloud:

you   up   look

Find the different words in each line.
e.g. Line 1: the different sound is in **bedroom**.

1	cup	dustbin	bedroom	lovely
2	roof	book	bathroom	too
3	blue	brush	new	you
4	thunder	look	put	notebook
5	museum	fun	instruction	cut

Answers

1 bedroom   2 bathroom   3 brush   4 thunder
5 museum

Have students say all the words aloud.

Transfer

Read this.

Students read silently.

This is a plan of a flat. It's on the fifth floor of a block of flats. There's a lift. In the flat, there's a living-room with a large window and a balcony. There's a kitchen. There isn't a dining room. There's a bathroom and a toilet. There's a large cupboard in the hall. There are two bedrooms.

If students are likely to find this difficult, check over the reading text with questions. These reproduce the text, allowing students to hear the words aloud.

e.g.
Is it on the third floor? Is it on the second floor? Which floor is it on?

Is there a lift? Is there a living-room? Is the window large or is it small? Is there a balcony? Is there a kitchen? Is there a bathroom? Is there a toilet? Is there a cupboard in the hall? Is it large or is it small? Are there three bedrooms? Are there four bedrooms? How many bedrooms are there?

Describe your home to your partner.

This is a free activity. You might have to provide further vocabulary as needed. e.g. *dining-room, garage, garden.*

Warning: Be aware that this activity will reveal differences in wealth. You may wish to avoid going too far into it.

2 Ask and answer about your town.

Students ask and answer in pairs or groups. This might involve adding necessary vocabulary throughout. If you think vocabulary will be a major problem, we suggest doing this as a whole class activity **before** the pair work. However, it would be preferable to do the pair work first and then open into a class discussion afterwards.

● *Where is it?*
■ *It's in the (north / south / east / west / centre) of (our country).*

Draw the points of the compass on the board if this needs explanation.

● *How big is it?*
■ *It's (small / large). There are(two million) people in my town.*

You may want to check:

2,000,000 - two million
200,000 - two hundred thousand
20,000 - twenty thousand
2,000 - two thousand

● *What's your favourite building?*
■ *My favourite building is (the museum).*

You should be ready to provide appropriate vocabulary if necessary

e.g.

cathedral, church, temple, mosque, castle, office building

● *Where are the shops?*
■ *There are small shops (in my street). There's a large supermarket (outside the town).*

You should be ready to provide appropriate vocabulary if necessary

e.g.

shopping centre, shopping mall, in the town centre

● *Are there any cinemas?*
■ *There are (three) cinemas. / There aren't any cinemas.*
● *Are there any factories?*
■ *There are some factories (outside the town).*

See: Vocabulary, page 40, 2 Buildings

3 Where were you?
Look at the words in the box. Ask and answer questions with a partner.

Students should do this in pairs, and should try and remember their partner's answers in preparation for 4 below.

When?	last (Saturday) last night on Monday in July at 9 o'clock
Where?	at school at home on the bus at the cinema at a friend's house at the supermarket on holiday in (Wigan) in (West Wallaby Street)

● *Were you (at school) last (Saturday)?*
■ *Yes, I was / No, I wasn't.*
● *Where were you last night?*
■ *I was at home.*

See: Grammar, page 42, 1 *was, were*

4 Change partners. Ask and answer questions about your first partner.

Having completed both pairwork activities, check with rapid questions around the class.

● *Was she (at home) last (night)?*
■ *Yes, she was / No, she wasn't.*
● *Where was she last night?*
■ *She was at a friend's house.*

Vocabulary

1 Wallace's house

Students should read silently and work alone to add vocabulary items to the boxes.

Answers (clockwise from the top right corner)
window / window ledge / letter box / front door / gate / pavement / path / steps / dog flap / fence / wall / roof

Read this. Look at the **bold** words. Put them in the correct boxes on the picture.

Wallace's home is a house in West Wallaby Street. The **walls** are brick. There's a small front garden, and there's a wall round the garden with a green **fence** on it. The **gate** is open, and there's a **path** to the **front door**. There's a **letter box** and a **dog flap** in the door. There is a porch with a grey **roof**. There are two bottles of milk on the **steps**. In the picture we can see five **windows**. We can see the **window ledges** on the three upstairs windows. The house has got two floors. There is a **pavement** outside the house.

2 Buildings

Students read silently.

Read this.

Wallace lives in a small town in the north of England. In the picture, we can see a street with some shops, a cinema and a supermarket. There are four terraced houses, a detached house and two semi-detached houses. They have got chimneys and TV aerials.

We can see a tall block of flats behind the shops. There are 120 flats in the block. They are building a new office block. We can see the scaffolding and the yellow crane. There's a factory too. It has got a tall chimney.

Can you see the lamp-post on the left and the museum on the right?

This is sufficient as it stands, but you could ask students to correct these false statements.

e.g.
T: Wallace lives in a large town …
Student: Wallace lives in a small town …
T: … in the south of France.
Student: … in the north of England.

Continue:
We can see a street with some shops, a café and a discotheque.

There are forty terraced houses a detached house and three semi-detached houses.
They have got chimneys and television aerials on the roofs.
We can see a tall block of offices behind the shops.
There are 12 flats in the block.
They are building a new cinema.
We can see the scaffolding and a yellow crane.
There's a factory too. It has got a small chimney.

3 How high … ?

This is a bridge. It's seventy-five metres long, and it's four metres wide. It's twenty-five metres high.

Write three questions and answers with *How wide …? How long …?* and *How high …?*

Answers
How wide is it?   It's four metres wide.
How long is it?   It's seventy-five metres long.
How high is it?   It's twenty-five metres high.

4 Spelling
Look at this.

control → controlling
write → writing
watch → watching

Write the *-ing* forms of these verbs.

Answers

have – having	hold – holding
cut – cutting	leave – leaving
measure – measuring	come – coming
hide – hiding	move – moving
sleep – sleeping	eat – eating
go – going	decorate – decorating
do – doing	sit – sitting

Higher levels
You could explain why the letter doubles in *cutting, sitting*.
1) *cute, site* are words. Compare the sound *cut / cute sit / site*
(Noting that some of the action takes place on a building *site* and that *cute* is American English for *pretty*).
Then add these pronunciation examples:
mad / made, wit / white-, hot / hotel
When it is vowel-consonant-vowel the first vowel is longer.
So *siting* is vowel-consonant-vowel and has a different pronunciation. To preserve the vowel sound of *sit* we avoid vowel-consonant-vowel by doubling the consonant: *cutting, sitting, shopping*, etc.

4 Vocabulary notebook
Write translations. You can use your dictionary.

In most cases students will gain great advantage by using a monolingual dictionary with simplified English explanations. However, at this level a bilingual dictionary is the best for this exercise. You may wish to check that the correct translations are given for the word in its context in the episode.

You may wish to write in model translations here for reference.

above	----	hole	----
box	----	ledge	----
calamity	----	measure (v)	----
careful	----	move	----
chicken	----	museum	----
city	----	next	----
clever	----	no one	----
come down	----	notebook	----
control (v)	----	penknife	----
diamond	----	plan	----
dustbin	----	reasonable	----
exhibition	----	reward	----
flap (n)	----	roof	----
funny	----	seen	----
get out	----	shocking	----
go up	----	sure	----
help	----	tape measure	----
high	----	terms	----

thousand	----	were	----
tired	----	wide	----
wait	----	window	----
was	----	write	----

Grammar

See: Student's Book, page 42

You may wish to spend time going through this. If so, we would encourage activating the student's language by introducing drills, questions, etc.

Transcript

See: Student's Book, page 43

Episode 5

Wallace's Sleepwalk

Watching the video

The first exercise gives an opportunity for practising *going to (do)* for future reference. But it also gives more opportunities to revise *was / were* while recapitulating the story.

Before you watch

1 What's going to happen in episode five?
Look at the pictures. They are clues!

This will be a free activity, and students may find it hard to put their ideas into words. We suggest giving them time for pair / group discussion before talking the clues over with the class. Here are some ideas:

The penguin with the electric drill. In this picture, the penguin is going to take the controls off the techno-trousers.

The penguin is measuring the window. Is this the City Museum? Maybe the penguin's going to go through this window.

Gromit upside-down. The techno-trousers can go up walls, and they can go upside-down. Is the penguin going to send the techno-trousers up the wall?

Plan. There's a diamond exhibition at the City Museum. There's a famous blue diamond there. Is the penguin going to steal it?

Wanted poster. Gromit can't remember. But is this a chicken? Or is it the penguin with a funny hat on?

Penguin, box and rubber glove. The penguin is the chicken with a red rubber glove on his head! So, the penguin is a famous criminal.

Watch all of episode five.

After you watch

2 Were your ideas about episode five correct?

This should be a free activity. You can ask leading questions.

e.g.
Were all your ideas correct? Was your partner correct?

3 What are these things? Can you remember the words?

Answers (from left to right)

red rubber glove / crash helmet / burglar alarm / pincers / (a loose) tile

See: Vocabulary, page 51, 4 Vocabulary notebook

SECTION ONE	00.00 to 01.02

Before you watch

1 What's happening?
Complete the sentences with words from the box.

dressing   coming down   opening   sitting   falling
closing   going up   sliding down

Answers

The penguin is closing the door.
The weight is coming down.*
The bed is going up.
The trap doors are opening.
Gromit is sliding down the bed.
Gromit is falling through the hole and into the trousers.*
Gromit is sitting back-to-front.
The robot is dressing Gromit.

Note: *Falling and coming down* might seem interchangeable. To be very accurate, as the weight is part of a machine, it isn't really falling freely, it is coming down. Gromit's descent is unintentional, and *coming down* implies a degree of intention. However, it's your choice whether to accept alternatives. At this level both answers are 'good enough'.

Watch section one.

After you watch

In the pre-watching activity, students were describing pictures. Therefore Present continuous is the appropriate tense. In the post-watching activity, students are describing a sequence, so the Present simple becomes the appropriate tense. Both exercises are utilizing the same basic vocabulary.

2 What happens next?
Look at the chart. Make sentences.
e.g.

First the penguin closes the door.

Continue with the story. (Two columns are in the correct order. Which ones?)

Once students work this out, the exercise is reasonably easy. Column 1 (sequence words) and column 3 (verbs) are in the correct order. Remember that *then / next* are the same as far as this exercise goes. Use them as you wish, but we have used *then* for closely sequential actions and *next* when there is a more important change in the sequence. This is quite subtle. We suggest getting students to do this in pairs or groups before checking with the whole class.

First	Gromit	closes	the bed.
	the penguin	comes down	the trousers.
Next	the jam	goes up	the door.
Then	the bed	slides down	sleeves on
Gromit.			
	the weight	falls through	the jam.
	the robot	falls into	the face.
Finally	the spoon	falls onto	the hole.
		puts	the chair.
		puts	a pullover on Gromit.
		goes into	the air.
		flies through	
		hits Gromit in	

Model answers

First the penguin closes the door.
Then the weight comes down.
Then the bed goes up.
Next Gromit slides down the bed.
Then he falls through the hole.
Then he falls into the trousers.
Then he falls onto the chair.
Next the robot puts a pullover on Gromit.
Then the robot puts sleeves on Gromit.
Next the spoon goes into the jam.
Then the jam flies through the air.
Finally the jam hits Gromit in the face.

See: Grammar, page 52, 3 Sequences

We would prefer to go through this later, but if students have noticed the change of tense and are worried, you could briefly look at this now.

SECTION TWO 01.03 to 02.31

Watch section two.

After you watch

2 Complete the sentences with words from the box.

| up | across | along | over | past | onto | off |

Students work alone. Check with the class.

Answers
1 They're walking along a dark alley.
2 They're going straight up the wall.
3 They're going past the window.
4 The penguin's getting off.
5 Wallace is walking up the wall and onto the roof.
6 Across the roof!
7 Up, and over and down.

The diagrams in the Grammar section will provide information for self-checking by students.

See: Grammar, page 52,
1 Adverbs of movement, prepositions

SECTION THREE 02.32 to 4.55

Before you watch

1 Look at the twenty-four pictures around this page. How many of the words do you know?

The words are listed under 2. There is no right answer, but encourage them to guess from mother tongue knowledge – things like *Tyrannosaurus Rex* sound difficult, but as they are the official Latin names they are international. The nationalities may help. Other things will be known from films. The word *stuffed* features – this is the art of taxidermy.

2 Can you remember? How many of these things are there inside the museum? Tick (✔) them.

This requires detailed observation – and depends to a degree on the resolution of your TV monitor! For example, we found it hard to see on some TVs that the Egyptian mummy also has a mummified guitar! On a reasonable monitor it is clear. It is fairest to make this a discussion rather than right or wrong.

Answers (clockwise)

Tyrannosaurus Rex skeleton ✔
painting ✔
Plesiosaurus skeleton ✔
Chinese vase ✔
Neanderthal man ✗
stuffed lion ✔
treasure chest ✗
Egyptian mummy ✔
gun ✗
mammoth ✔
model ship ✗
Roman pots ✔
stuffed penguins ✔
Egyptian papyrus ✔
abbacus ✗
model dinosaurs ✔
shield and axes ✔
Greek statue ✗
guitar ✔
suit of armour ✔
club ✔
diamond ✔
Egyptian cat ✔
pillar ✔

While you watch

3 What can you see?
Check your answers to 2.

You will probably want to replay the video, pausing to
note details.

Watch section three.

After you watch

**4 Work with a partner. Number these sentences
in order from 1 to 12.**

2 Air vent, long room, diamond room. Stop here.
6 He's over!
3 It's the blue diamond.
11 A loose tile!
8 Forward. Try again.
1 Through the air vent, and into the museum.
12 Mind the laser beam.
9 Got it! Slowly! ... oh! Yes!
4 Forward. Across the ceiling.
5 There's a burglar alarm, with laser beams.
7 Pincers. Back ... down ... missed!
10 That was lucky.

Students should self-correct by comparing their answers
with the Transcript on page 53.

5 Who's doing it?
Match the questions to the pictures.

Answers
1 Who's yawning? B
2 Who's wiping his forehead? C
3 Who's sweating? A

**Then ask and answer questions about section
three.**

Students should try to ask questions with *Who?*. If they
naturally move to other questions, let them.
It's impossible to predict all the questions. They can
obviously ask all three questions above. For weaker
classes this will be quite sufficient.

Watch section three without sound.

6 Tell the story.
**Work in pairs. Watch section three again
without sound. Close your book, and describe
what's happening to your partner.**
e.g.

*I can see inside the museum. There are two dinosaurs.
Wallace is coming through the air vent ...*

This is a free activity. The use of prepositions and
adverbs of movement is what we are hoping for, though.
After the pairwork, you could either get a student to
model the sequence with the video, or you could model
it yourself. Play the video without sound and give a
model commentary.

SECTION FOUR   04.56 to 06.04

Before you watch

1 Number the pictures in order from 1 to 8.
Answers
A 2 / B 4 / C 7 / D 1 / E 5 / F 3 / G 8 / H 6

Watch section four.

After you watch

**2 Match these sentences to the pictures.
Number them from 1 to 8.**

Preferably, have students discuss this in pairs so that
they complete the task together. Check with the class.
e.g.
T: Which one's first?
Student 1: The burglar alarm goes off.
T: Is she correct?
Student 2: Yes, she is.
T: Are you certain?
Student 2: Yes, I am. etc.

Answers
2 Wallace has got one foot on the ceiling, and one foot
on the loose tile.
5 The window turns over.
7 Wallace walks down the wall.
1 The burglar alarm goes off.
8 Wallace is in the alley.
3 The alarm wakes Wallace up.
6 The penguin gets onto Wallace's back.
4 The automatic security door closes.

3 Where's the diamond at the end of the story?

Ask students to give their ideas. They will probably have to watch the sequence again to be sure.

Answers

It's still in the museum.
It's inside the crash helmet.
The penguin's holding it. ✔

4 Tell the story.

This is another free, open activity where fluency rather than accuracy is the aim. Having done the exercises, students should generate Present simple to explain the sequence, but as long as they can describe it in their own words, it is sufficient.

Work with a partner and tell the story of section four. The sentences in 2 above tell some of the story. Add more sentences and tell all the story.

Watch all of episode five again.

Exercises

1 Memory

Are these sentences true (✔) or false (✗)?

Answers

1 The pincers are inside the crash helmet. ✔
2 Wallace is wearing tartan pyjamas over the techno-trousers. ✗
3 There isn't any toast in the toaster. ✔
4 The penguin gets onto the window ledge. ✔
5 The diamond is in the Long Room. ✗
6 The diamond is on a blue and yellow cushion. ✗
7 The pincers get the diamond the first time. ✗
8 There are two loose tiles on the ceiling. ✔

Now correct the false sentences.

Answers

2 Wallace is wearing striped pyjamas over the techno-trousers.
5 The diamond is in the Diamond Room.
6 The diamond is on a red and yellow cushion.
  or
  The diamond is on a red and gold cushion.
(This depends on whether students know *gold* or not. Both are acceptable.)
7 The pincers get the diamond the second time.

> **Higher levels**
> **Check that the students stress the altered words – those in bold above – when saying the corrected sentences.**

2 Test yourself
Choose the correct word in (brackets).

Answers

1 (What / Why)'s the crash helmet for?
2 What's he going (do / to do) with the controls?
3 Poor Wallace is (still / yet) asleep.
4 (Mind / Be careful) the laser beam!
5 This is a (badly / bad) dream.
6 What are (those / these) lights?
7 (I'm / I) afraid of heights.
8 It's (again / against) the law.

Now check with the Transcript on page 53.

Have students self-check before you give correct answers.

3 Nationalities
Look at the chart. Use words from the three columns.

e.g. *An Egyptian mummy*

a	Egyptian	Delight
an	French	tea
some	Italian	penknife
	Turkish	cosmonaut
	English	pizza
	Chinese	video game
	Swiss	jeans
	Russian	perfume
	American	vase
	Japanese	mummy

There aren't definite answers to this. For example, *Chinese tea, English tea, Japanese tea, Russian tea* will all work. The collocations might be personal opinion. But we have listed what we think are the most obvious answers, so that each word is used once only.

Possible answers

an Egyptian mummy
some French perfume
an Italian pizza
some Turkish Delight
some English tea
a Chinese vase
a Swiss penknife
a Russian cosmonaut
some American jeans
a Japanese video game

> **See also Higher Levels above for nationality groups (-ish, an, -ian, -ese, -i, irregular).**

This would be a good opportunity to revise *a/an* noting that they agree with the first letter of the next word (in this case an adjective), not with the noun. You could give a rapid oral drill.

e.g.
T: Italian pizza.
Student: An Italian pizza.

Continue: French perfume / Chinese vase / Egyptian mummy / American car / Turkish restaurant / Indian shirt, etc.

You could also check countables and uncountables – all the uncountables in the above list take *some*. This can also be drilled in the same way.

Can you think of some more examples?

This depends on the class. Here are a few (*food, restaurant, car* also work for most of them):

An American plane, T-shirt / a Japanese TV, hi-fi, video / some Swiss chocolate / a Swiss watch / some Chinese food / some Greek yoghurt / some Turkish coffee, yoghurt / a Polish car / some Italian spaghetti / an Italian suit / a French dress / a German car / some Spanish wine / a Mexican wave (at a football match) / a Brazilian footballer

4 Sounds
Look at the words in the box. Match the words with the same sounds.

e.g. *dream / beam*

heights	dream	law	loose	glove	again
wall	roof	rubber	lights	afraid	beam

Answers
heights / lights
law / wall
loose / roof
glove / rubber
again / afraid

Have students say all the words aloud.

Higher levels
You can choose whether to introduce phonetics with this exercise.

Transfer

1 Giving directions

Make sure students begin at *You are here*.

Look at the map. You are giving directions to the school. Complete the sentences with words from the box.

right	left	past	over	straight on

Answers
Turn left and go past the supermarket. Go over the bridge across the railway. Go straight on. Go past the statue. Take the third road on the right. The school is at the end of the road.

The Grammar references may seem daunting, but it gives students cover of all the necessary words together with diagrams. You could point out the spellings, *straight, right, eight, night, light* (+ *height, bright, fight, knight* – see the museum, at higher levels). You could ask students to spell them.

e.g.
T: Can you spell 'straight'?
Student 1: Yes. S-T-R-A-I-G-H-T.

See: Grammar, page 52, 1 Adverbs of movement and prepositions;

also: Grammar, page 42, 5 Prepositions and adverbs;

and: Grammar, page 12, 5 *Where is it?*

2 Work with a partner. Look at the map.
Student A

Give directions:
1 to the bank
2 to the museum
3 to the shops
4 from the school to the zoo
Then ask 'Where are you?'

Student B

Turn your book round.

Give directions:
1 to the zoo
2 to the slide in the park
3 to the building site
4 from the station to the museum
Then ask 'Where are you?'

This is a free activity. The model answers are not the only possibilities. You could find different routes to the same places.

Model answers
A – to the bank
Turn left and go past the supermarket. Go over the bridge across the railway (*or* Go across the bridge over the railway.). Turn right. Go past the shops. The bank is on the left near the park.

A – to the museum
Turn left and go past the supermarket. Go over the bridge across the railway (*or* Go across the bridge over the railway.). Take the second road on the right. Go through the gate and into the park. Go up the steps (up the hill) to the museum.

A – to the shops
Turn left and go past the supermarket. Go over the bridge across the railway (*or* Go across the bridge over the railway). Take the first road on the right. The shops are on the left (of the road).

A – from the school to the zoo
Go out of the school and turn left. Go past the statue and take the second road on the left. Go past the shops and the station. The shops are on the left and the station is on the right. The bank is on the left. Go past the bank. The gate to the zoo is on the left.

B – to the zoo
Turn left and go past the supermarket. Go over the bridge across the railway (*or* Go across the bridge over the railway.). Turn right. Go past the shops and the bank. The gate to the zoo is on the left.

B – to the slide in the park
Turn left and go past the supermarket. Go over the bridge across the railway (*or* Go across the bridge over the railway.). Take the second road on the right. Go through the gate and into the park. The slide is on the right.

B – to the building site
Turn left and go past the supermarket. Go over the bridge across the railway (or Go across the bridge over the railway.). Take the first road on the left. The building site is on the right.

B – from the station to the museum (on the map, the station only has an exit road on one side).
Go out of the station and turn left. Go over the small bridge (footbridge) across the railway. Turn left. Go past the shops. Turn right. Take the first road on the right. Go past the statue and through the gate and into the park. Go up the steps (up the hill) to the museum.

3 Work with a partner.

1 Give directions to rooms in this school.
2 Give directions to places near the school.

This is a free fluency activity.

Vocabulary

1 Inside the museum
Look at the pictures, and complete the texts.

Though this exercise appears hard, it is only a matter of looking back at page 46 where the items are labelled.

Answers
The Long Room
The air vent is in the ceiling on the right of the Long Room. Below it, there is a glass case with some old Roman pots. They are two thousand years old. There is a blue and white Chinese vase on top of the case. It is five hundred years old. On the wall there is a large painting by a famous British painter. There are two dinosaur skeletons. On the right there is a Tyrannosaurus Rex. It is sixty-five million years old. In the middle there is a Plesiosaurus.
In front of this dinosaur, there are some stuffed penguins in a glass case. Behind the dinosaur, there is another glass case. There are some small model dinosaurs in it.
On the left, there is a mammoth skeleton. It is thirty thousand years old. Behind the mammoth, there is a stuffed lion in a glass case.

The Diamond Room
The Blue Diamond is in the middle of the room. It is on a red cushion. The cushion is on top of a small pillar. There are some ropes around the pillar.
There are two tall pillars. One is on the left of the doorway, and the other is on the right of the doorway. There are statues of cats on top of the pillars. They are Egyptian.
There is a suit of armour on the right of the doorway. It is six hundred years old. Above it there is a shield and two axes. On the left of the doorway, there is an Egyptian mummy.
On the left there is a glass case with some masks in it. They are from the Pacific islands. Above the case, there is a club. There is a guitar next to the case. Maybe it is the mummy's guitar! There is some Egyptian papyrus on the wall above the guitar. The writing on the papyrus is four thousand years old.

For vocabulary, see: Watching the Video, page 46

Higher levels
You could extend practice on *four hundred years old*, etc.
e.g.
My sister is five years old. / This town is two thousand years old. / This puppy is six months old. / It's three weeks old. / It's five days old.

2 Large numbers
Match the numbers with the words.

Answers
one hundred thousand – 100,000
one thousand – 1000
one million – 1,000,000
one hundred – 100
ten thousand – 10,000

Look at this.

Have students say these aloud.

192 – *one hundred and ninety-two*
1850 – *one thousand eight hundred and fifty*
32,000 – *thirty-two thousand*
290,000 – *two hundred and ninety thousand*
1,450,000 – *one million four hundred and fifty thousand*

Write these numbers in words.

Answers
489 – four hundred and eighty-nine
3761 – three thousand seven hundred and sixty-one
15,824 – fifteen thousand eight hundred and twenty-four
125,555 – one hundred and twenty-five thousand five hundred and fifty-five
1,750,000 – one million seven hundred and fifty thousand
25,000,000 – twenty-five million

Having done the exercise, tell students to underline the word *and* in each example.

Higher levels
We use <u>commas</u> not <u>points</u> to seperate large numbers. You will also see spaces instead of commas: *1 000 000 / 25 354 000*, but this is irritating on computers which see the spaces as seperating different numbers. On computers it is generally easier to put nothing at all, and the use of computers is changing the way we write numbers too. A computer prefers *1345000*. Even in writing it is rarer to seperate four figure numbers nowadays. Both *1,000* and *1000* are common. (See *3761* in the exercise). In English, <u>points</u> seperate numbers from decimal fractions: *1.75*. In writing the point is put above the line, but in typing it goes on the line. Points are also called <u>full stops</u> in punctuation (American English: *periods*)

3 Words to remember?
There are a lot of new words in this episode.
Maybe you can't remember all the new words.

Write down ten words that you want to learn.

One of the most important points in 'learning how to learn' and acquiring study skills is to be able to discard or reject what you do not need to know. No one can learn everything, and the rather unusual vocabulary items in the museum can be used to demonstrate this. Few students really need to know all these words. They should review the vocabulary items in the unit and decide which ones are worth remembering and which ones can be discarded. (By the way, if the teacher says 'Don't remember this word' then the teacher is almost guaranteeing that the word will be the only one they do remember!)

4 Vocabulary notebook
Write translations. You can use your dictionary.

In most cases students will gain great advantage by using a monolingual dictionary with simplified English explanations. However, at this level a bilingual dictionary is the best for this exercise. You may wish to check that the correct translations are given for the word in its context in the episode.

You may wish to write in model translations here for reference.

air vent		loose	
alley		lucky	
automatic		mind (v)	
burglar alarm		pincers	
close		place	
crash helmet		put on	
cushion		robot	
dark		rubber	
dream		security door	
fall		sleeve	
forehead		slide (v)	
fly		sweat	
get off		tile	
glove		trap door	
heights		wake up	
hit		weight	
hole		wipe	
laser beam		yawn	
law			

Grammar

See: Student's Book, page 52

You may wish to spend time going through this. If so, we would encourage activating the student's language by introducing drills, questions, etc.

Transcript

See: Student's Book, page 53

41

Stop that train!

Watching the video

This episode has only three sections.

Even if you prefer splitting the video into sections without watching the whole episode first, we would suggest that you play the whole of episode 6 without stopping initially. Students will be caught up in the dynamic of the story and keen to get to the end.

Before you watch

**1 What's going to happen?
Choose three possible endings for the story.**

Answers
Wallace is going to go to prison.
The penguin is going to live in Antarctica.
Gromit is going to find a new owner.
The penguin is going to escape on a train. ✔
The diamond is going to return to the museum. ✔
Wallace is going to get a reward. ✔
The penguin is going to shoot Gromit.
Gromit is going to get his bedroom back. ✔
Wallace is going to sell the techno-trousers for a lot of money.
There is going to be a happy ending. ✔

We have ticked the five true answers above. The 'right answer' is not yet relevant though. It's the students' opinions that count, and it's language practice whatever they think. Have them discuss in pairs and groups then discuss with the class.

> **Higher levels**
> **They could be asked to give reasons for their choices.**

Watch all of episode six.

After you watch

2 Were your ideas right?

At this point you can check the answers.

Before you watch

1 What happens next?

Look at pictures 1 to 4.

What happens after each picture? Match them with pictures A to D.

This exercise is done from memory.

Answers
1 C / 2 D / 3 B / 4 A

Watch section one.

After you watch

2 Look at the pictures and connect the sentences.

Answers
The penguin takes off the rubber glove then Wallace says, 'Penguin! It's you.'
Gromit has got a rolling pin but the penguin has got a gun.
Gromit puts the electric wires together and the feet on the techno-trousers move up and down.
The wardrobe is going to fall onto Gromit so Gromit jumps onto the lampshade.

> See: Grammar, page 62, *and, but, so, then*

> **Higher levels**
> **This point can be explained, though we would leave this until later in the exploitation of the episode.**

Before you watch

Use the diagram to check vocabulary. Then have the students complete the exercise. Check with the class. The distinction between *shoots, hits* and *misses* will be important for telling the story later.

**1 A good shot
Complete the sentences with *shoots, hits* and *misses*.**

Answers
The penguin is a good shot. He shoots eight times.
The first shot hits the lampshade wire and breaks it.
Then he shoots at Gromit but he misses him.
The third shot hits the lampshade on Gromit's head.
The fourth shot hits the penguin flap and breaks it.
He shoots three times at Wallace and Gromit. One shot misses, but two of the shots hit the lampshade.
The next shot hits the lever and changes the points. Wallace is now on a different track. He takes the penguin's gun from him.

> See: Vocabulary, page 60, 1 Trains

Watch section one.

After you watch

2 Who gets stuck? Make true sentences.

We practise this at length, not because *to get stuck* is a vitally important verb, but because they will need to be able to express this for telling the story. Students could do this in pairs. Check with the class.

Wallace	gets	stuck	in	the wardrobe.
The penguin			on	the techno-trousers.
The wardrobe				the moose's head.
The net				the bedroom doorway.
				the serving hatch.
The techno-trousers	get			the bottle.

Model answers
Wallace gets stuck in the techno-trousers.
The penguin gets stuck in the bottle.
The wardrobe gets stuck in the bedroom doorway.
The net gets stuck on the moose's head.
The techno-trousers get stuck in the serving hatch.

> See: Vocabulary, page 61, 2 Things in the house

There are some unusual items on show in the video, and again students will need to be able to name them.

3 Where do they land?
Complete the sentences with *Wallace, Gromit* or *the penguin*.

This exercise is also designed to teach vocabulary items needed for telling the story.

Answers
The penguin slides down the banister and lands in the coal tender.
Gromit falls from the lampshade and lands on a coach.
Wallace flies through the serving hatch and lands on a vegetable trolley.
The penguin flies through the air and lands in a bottle.

> **Higher levels**
> As in Episode 5, you could ask students which words they think they will want to remember. There are some obvious examples of words which should be understood passively rather than committed to memory.

| SECTION THREE | 03.17 to 04.54 |

Before you watch

Ask and answer these questions.

Answers
What is the penguin's name?
The penguin's name is Feathers McGraw.

Where is the penguin now?
The penguin is in the zoo.

Is this his first time 'inside'?
No, it isn't.

The newspaper says that Feathers McGraw is back inside. *Inside* is an idiomatic way of saying in prison, though in this case it's the zoo, not prison. If he is back inside, then he was inside before. So it is not his first time.

> **Higher levels**
> You could expand this with examples.
> e.g.
> *I'm going back to England. Was I in England before?*
> *That café is very good. I'm going back there.*
> *You haven't got your book. Go back home and get it.*

Watch section three.

After you watch

1 What does Wallace say?
Match the sentences to the pictures.

Students work alone and compare answers with a partner.

Answers
B We've got one thousand pounds reward.
C I'd like a nice piece of cheese.
D A nice cup of tea and a piece of cheese!
A Thank you, old friend.

2 Ask and answer these questions.

Have students ask and answer the questions in pairs. Check with the class.

Answers
1 Is Wallace putting the money in the piggy-bank?
   No, he isn't.
2 What is Wallace eating?
   He's eating cheese / some cheese.
3 Is Gromit reading the newspaper?
   No, he isn't.
4 What is Gromit doing?
   He's looking at the techno-trousers. / He's watching the techno-trousers. / He's looking out of the window.
5 What are the techno-trousers doing?
   They're going / walking past the window. / They're escaping.

You could add questions (remembering that *I don't know.* is a valid answer).

e.g.
Where were the techno-trousers? (They were in the dustbin.)
Is someone controlling them?
Are Wallace and Gromit going to see them again?
Is the penguin going to get out of the zoo?

Watch all of episode six again.

After you watch

Tell the story of episode six. Use the pictures on the next page. Add other information. You can look at the pictures on pages 54 to 56 too.

They should try this in pairs first. An initial task would be to number the pictures in order. This will involve some discussion. Then they can tell the story. Then get students to reproduce the story in class. After each student has said a sentence or two, move on to another student selected at random.

Watch all of *The Wrong Trousers*. Don't stop the tape. Talk about the story after you watch.

This will take thirty minutes, so in most situations it would have to be done in a later lesson. We consider it absolutely essential that students should experience the whole story so as to see how much their comprehension has improved, and also for the opportunity of watching something in English without stopping for this length of time. Talk about the story might involve retelling the whole story, or it might involve talking about their reactions to it. With some classes, it might even involve talking about claymation and the animation techniques which are used.

Exercises

1 Memory
Are these sentences true (✔) or false (✗)?

Answers
1 The penguin puts the red glove into the sack. ✗
2 Wallace puts the electric wires together. ✗
3 The penguin slides down the banister. ✔
4 The kitchen wallpaper is green with clouds on. ✗
5 The spare track is in a red and yellow box. ✔
6 The railway track goes under the table. ✔
7 The penguin lands in a teapot. ✗
8 Gromit's new collar and lead are on the penguin. ✔
9 The penguin goes to prison. ✗

Now correct the false sentences.

Answers
1 The penguin puts the diamond into the sack.
2 Gromit puts the electric wires together.
4 The kitchen wallpaper is blue with clouds on.
or
4 The kitchen wallpaper is light blue with clouds on.
7 The penguin lands in a bottle.
9 The penguin goes to the zoo.

> **Higher levels**
> Check that the students stress the altered words – those in bold above – when saying the corrected sentences.

2 Test yourself
Choose the correct word in (brackets).

Answers
1 The penguin ('s got / got) a gun.
2 The wardrobe's (lock / locked) now.
3 The train's (in / on) time.
4 Give it to (me / my).
5 He's getting (across / away).
6 He (hasn't / haven't) got an engine.
7 I (like / 'd like) a nice piece of cheese.
8 They (can't / don't) escape.
9 I am (enjoying / enjoy) this cheese.

Now check with the Transcript on page 63.

Have students self-check before you give correct answers.

3 *box, bottle, piece, cup*
How many words can you add to the chart?

This is open. They can add other things from their own knowledge. We've just added two obvious suggestions per column.

cup	box	bottle	piece
a cup of tea	a box of spare track	a bottle of milk	a piece of cheese
a cup of coffee	a box of dog food	a bottle of water	a piece of bread
a cup of chocolate	a box of Kleenex	a bottle of lemonade	a piece of apple

4 Sounds
Look at these words from episode six. Find the word in each line with the different vowel sound,
e.g. Line 1: The different sound is in **wardrobe**

1	spare	there	wardrobe	where
2	net	break	engine	help
3	open	shot	bottle	controls
4	thief	escape	cheese	piece
5	reward	lampshade	straight	station
6	crash	track	catch	dark
7	pin	mind	little	penguin
8	minute	nice	right	time

Answers
1 wardrobe
2 break
3 open
4 cheese
5 reward
6 dark
7 mind
8 time

Have students say all the words aloud.

> **Higher levels**
> You can choose whether to introduce phonetics with this exercise.

Transfer

1 What would you like?

In traditional text books *would like* was taught late, because it was considered to be a conditional sentence. In recent textbooks, it is taught early on because it can be taught as a fixed formula without ever mentioning conditionals. In fact, it is easy to manipulate as it is exactly the same in all persons ... *I'd / You'd / He'd / She'd / We'd / They'd*. You could reinforce this with some rapid substitution drills. As students will find it difficult to hear the d in *I'd like*, have them begin by repeating in these stages:

I / I'd / I'd like / I'd like a T-shirt.

Do the drills, chorally at first. Then with individual students selected at random.

T: I.
Student: I'd like a T-shirt.
Continue: She /We / I / They / He / You

T: You.
Student: Would you like a drink?
Continue: they / he / it / we / she / I

T: I.
Student: I wouldn't like a T-shirt.
Continue: he / they / you / she / we

You might also check the use of *a / an* versus *some*.

Ask and answer questions.

● *Would you like a T-shirt for your birthday?*
■ *Yes, I would.*

● *Would you like some bubble bath for your birthday?*
■ *No, I wouldn't*

Students should note / remember their partners answers in preparation for the next activity.

2 Change partners. Ask and answer questions about your first partner.

● *Would she like a T-shirt for her birthday?*
■ *Yes, she would.*

● *Would she like some bubble bath for her birthday?*
■ *No, she wouldn't.*

Then ask students about the illustrated items in a conversational way.
e.g.

T: Maria, would you like some bubble-bath?
Student 1: Yes, I would.
T: Ask Paul.
Student 1: Paul, would you like some bubble bath?
Student 2: No, I wouldn't.
T: Anna, ask Dan about a T-shirt.
Student 3: Would you like a T-shirt, Dan?
Student 4: Yes, I would.
T: (indicates S5) Ask me.
Student 5: Would you like a T-shirt?
T: Yes, I would.

Add other items as appropriate.

3 Class survey.
Ask three students these questions.

This is totally open. Encourage students to answer truthfully. They can note the replies.

1 Who's your favourite character in 'The Wrong Trousers'?

❏ Wallace   ❏ Gromit   ❏ The penguin

2 Which is your favourite episode?

❏ 1 Gromit's birthday

❏ 2 Room to let

❏ 3 Wallace, Gromit and the penguin

❏ 4 The Penguin's plan

❏ 5 Wallace's sleepwalk

❏ 6 Stop that train!

3 Give examples of:

❏ an easy episode (the English was easy)

❏ a difficult episode (the English was difficult)

❏ a sad episode

❏ an exciting episode

4 How much of English in 'The Wrong Trousers' do you understand now?

❏ nearly everything (90% +)

❏ a lot of it (75% +)

❏ about half (50%)

❏ under half (30%)

❏ nothing

Check by asking about the replies they received.
e.g.

Which is Maria's favourite episode?
Whose favourite character is the penguin?
Which is a sad episode for you, Paul?
Do you understand nearly everything, Anna?
etc.

Vocabulary

1 Trains
Look at the bold words. Put them in the correct boxes on the pictures.

This is a railway train. The train is on a railway **track.** The blue **engine** is at the front of the train, with its **coal tender.** The penguin is sitting on the coal tender. Gromit is on one of the red **coaches.** There are three **wagons** at the end of the train. Wallace is standing on the last wagon. The penguin is holding a **pin.** The pin connects the engine to the coaches.

The engine is going straight along the **track.** Wallace and Gromit are on the coaches. They are going to change direction and go along another track. There is a **signal** between the tracks. **Points** change the direction from one railway track to another railway track.

One of the points on Wallace's model railway is electric. The switch is a **red button.** The other points aren't electric. The switches are levers.

Answers (begin at the top left and go round clockwise)
coaches / wagons / track / pin / lever / red button / points / track / signal / tender / engine

2 Things in the house

This section is purely for reference.

The **key** is in the **lock** in the **wardrobe** door.

There is a **serving hatch** between the kitchen and the dining-room.

Wallace is on the **vegetable trolley.** He's trying to catch the penguin with a **net.**

The net gets stuck on a **moose's head.**

The penguin gets stuck in a milk **bottle.** Gromit catches the **sack** with the diamond in it.

3 Vocabulary notebook
Write translations. You can use your dictionary.

In most cases students will gain great advantage by using a monolingual dictionary with simplified English explanations. However, at this level a bilingual dictionary is the best for this exercise. You may wish to check that the correct translations are given for the word in its context in the episode.

You may wish to write in model translations here for reference.

banister		engine	
break / breaks		escape	
brilliant		fall / falls	
broken		fly / flies	
catch / catches		friend	
cheese		get away	
coach		get out of	

get stuck		prison	
gun		reward	
hit / hits		rolling-pin	
key		sack	
lampshade		shoot/ shoots	
land / lands		shot	
little		stay / stays	
locked		stuck	
miss/ misses		take / takes	
more		thief	
net		track	
old		wagon	
piece		wardrobe	
pin		way	
points		zoo	
police station			

Grammar

See: Student's Book, page 62

You may wish to spend time going through this. If so, we would encourage activating the student's language by introducing drills, questions, etc.

Transcript

See: Student's Book, page 63

Notes